Charles A. Story

Alcohol, its Nature and Effects

Ten Lectures

Charles A. Story

Alcohol, its Nature and Effects
Ten Lectures

ISBN/EAN: 9783743427624

Manufactured in Europe, USA, Canada, Australia, Japa

Cover: Foto ©Lupo / pixelio.de

Manufactured and distributed by brebook publishing software (www.brebook.com)

Charles A. Story

Alcohol, its Nature and Effects

ITS

NATURE AND EFFECTS.

TEN LECTURES.

BY
DR. CHARLES A. STORY,
OF CHICAGO.

NEW YORK:
National Temperance Society and Publication House,
172 WILLIAM STREET.
1868.

Entered, according to Act of Congress, in the year 1868, by

J. N. STEARNS,

In the Clerk's Office of the District Court for the Eastern District of New York.

ROCKWELL & ROLLINS, STEREOTYPERS AND PRINTERS,
122 Washington Street, Boston.

PREFACE.

PEOPLE OF THE GREAT REPUBLIC! You are masters of a land over which no monarch rules. You are the owners and governors of a soil which requires only wisdom, watchfulness, and perseverance to make it eternally free. Any cause that you espouse will soon be successful in fact, and famous in history. Your wishes and desires soon change into established policy, and your policy becomes the law. Let liberty inspire your counsels, and justice preside over all your acts. These Lectures may, perhaps, help to inform your judgment, and inspire your zeal. Rulers in the Land of the Free! I dedicate them to you and to your posterity. If you have faith in a holy cause, and trust in each other, all will be well.

CHARLES A. STORY, M. D.

CHICAGO, ILL. April, 1868.

CONTENTS.

I.

THE NATURE OF ALCOHOL — WHERE DOES IT COME FROM? — HOW CAN YOU GET IT? — HOW MUCH IS THERE IN THE LIQUOR? — WHAT IS IT GOOD FOR? — AND WHAT IS IT? 7

II.

THE NATURE OF ALCOHOL — WHERE DOES IT COME FROM? — HOW CAN YOU GET IT? — HOW MUCH IS THERE IN THE LIQUOR? — WHAT IS IT GOOD FOR? — AND WHAT IS IT? 51

III.

ALCOHOL — WHAT EFFECT HAS IT UPON THE HUMAN BODY? — DOES IT EVER CAUSE DISEASE AND DEATH? — WHAT PART OF THE SYSTEM DOES IT INJURE? — HOW AND WHY? 89

IV.

Alcohol — What Effect has it upon the Human Body? — Does it ever cause Disease and Death? — What Part of the System does it Injure? — How and Why?   185

V.

Alcohol — What Effect has it upon the Immortal Mind? — Does it ever cause Indolence, Ignorance, or Depravity? — Is it ever the Cause of Mania, Insanity, Madness, Lunacy, Delirium, Wickedness, or Crime? — Does it increase the Number of Dolts, Idiots, and Fools? — In what Way? — and why?   175

VI.

Alcohol — What Effect has it upon the Immortal Mind? — Does it ever cause Indolence, Ignorance, or Depravity? — Is it ever the Cause of Mania, Insanity, Madness, Lunacy, Delirium, Wickedness, or Crime? — Does it in-

CREASE THE NUMBER OF DOLTS, IDIOTS,
AND FOOLS?—IN WHAT WAY?—AND
WHY? 221

VII.

ALCOHOL—HOW MUCH IS MADE?—HOW
MANY FACTORIES?—HOW MUCH GRAIN
AND FRUIT IS USED IN MAKING IT?—HOW
MANY PEOPLE ARE THUS EMPLOYED?—IN
HOW MANY PLACES IS IT KEPT FOR SALE?
—HOW MANY PEOPLE DRINK IT?—HOW
SOON DO THE VICTIMS DIE?—HOW MANY
YEARS OF HUMAN LIFE ARE WASTED?—
HOW GREAT IS THE NUMBER OF THE DEAD?
—HOW MANY DRINKERS ARE REFORMED?
—AND WHO? 269

VIII.

ALCOHOL—ITS RESULTS REDUCED TO DOLLARS
AND CENTS.—WHAT IS THE VALUE OF THE
TIME AND INDUSTRY LOST?—HOW MUCH
MONEY DOES IT TAKE TO MAINTAIN HOSPITALS FOR DRUNKEN VAGABONDS?—WHAT
IS THE COST OF ASYLUMS FOR LUNATICS
AND IDIOTS?—WHAT IS THE COST OF
CRIMES AND PRISONS?—HOW MUCH DO
WE PAY OUR PAUPERS?—WHAT IS THE
VALUE OF THE PROPERTY WE BURN AND
DESTROY?—WHO PAYS THE TAXES?—

Does this accord with Justice, Liberty, and Law? 305

IX.

Alcohol — Is it ever adulterated or counterfeited? — What are some of the Substances used in its Adulteration? — Are any of these Substances poison? — What are organic vegetable Alkalies? — Are they cheaper than Alcohol itself? — How much cheaper? — To what Extent are alcoholic Liquors adulterated? — Is it a Crime to put deadly Poisons in Liquors? . . . 329

X.

Alcohol — Are there many Articles used in imitating it? — What are Some of them? — To what Extent is Adulteration carried on? — How do you know? — Have you got any responsible Authorities? — Who? — Any Books? — What Books? — Can you detect these Frauds? — How? — What about Chemistry? — Should deliberate Fraud be punished? — What is the Duty of a free People? 361

I.

The Nature of Alcohol — Where does it come from? — How can you get it? — How Much is there in the Liquor? — What is it good for? — And what is it?

DIAGRAMS OF THE STOMACH IN VARIOUS CONDITIONS.

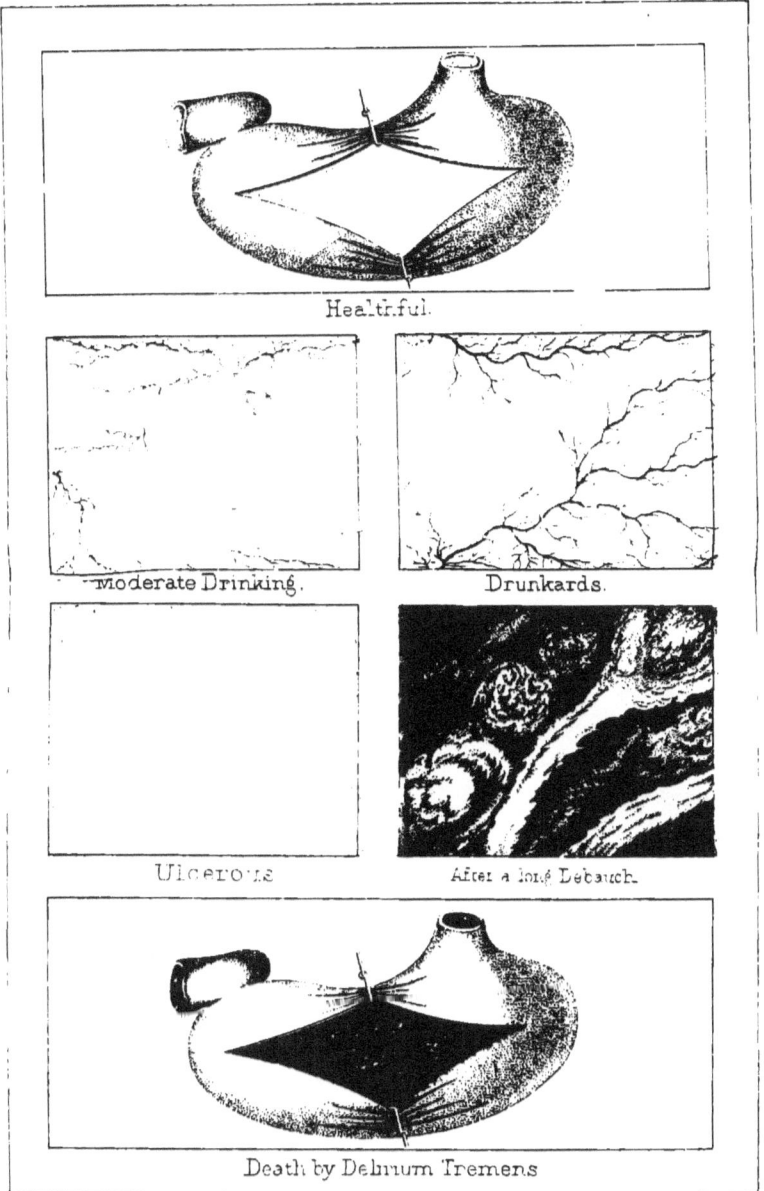

ALCOHOL;
ITS NATURE AND EFFECTS.

I.

We live in a Republic, where the people are supreme, where the majority rules, and where public opinion is the foundation of law.

To educate the public mind, and to awaken the public conscience, concerning a given subject, is equivalent to enacting laws upon that subject; because out of the mind and heart of the people the laws of the land are made.

The trickery and chicanery of the selfish and avaricious cannot long prevail against a just and righteous cause, upon which the people are well educated. And the Temperance cause will be triumphant only when the people are thoroughly informed upon the subject.

All information given to the people should be principles and facts, drawn from standard medical and legal works, and other reliable sources of authority.

Such information, thus obtained, will have more weight on the mind of the people than mere eloquence, and do more to convince them that the cause of Temperance is just and worthy, than any other form of appeal.

Theory and fancy do very well for ornament, but argument is worth more than rhetoric only, and facts have more value than high-sounding words.

The first inquiries that present themselves are concerning alcohol:—

Where do we find it?

How is it obtained? and

What is it good for?

In answering these questions, let me call your attention to the "United States Dispensatory;" a book written by Dr. George B. Wood, of Philadelphia, and adopted as a standard work of authority by all the druggists, and all the regular physicians throughout the Republic.

You will find this book in all the respectable drug-stores in the land, and all the doctors will tell you it is reliable authority.

From an article on alcohol, on page 60 of that work, I shall make a number of extracts : —

"Alcohol is the intoxicating ingredient in all spirituous liquors, including, under this term, wines, porter, ale, beer, cider, and every other liquid which has undergone the vinous fermentation."

What does it say? "Alcohol is the intoxicating ingredient in all spiritous liquors." So says Dr. Wood; and no intelligent man will undertake to deny him as authority. He has been at the head of the medical faculty of Philadelphia, and regarded as a first-class chemist, for half a century; and during that time has revised his Dispensatory every five years, adding to it and taking from it, as science and the discovery of new truths have directed. The quotations I make have stood the test of advancing science and criticism for fifty years!

He says: "Alcohol is the intoxicating ingredient in all spirituous liquors;" but he means all pure spirituous liquors, of course, because he was not then considering the vile adulterations, filthy compounds, base counterfeits, and imitations, that we frequently find in the liquor market. We are speaking in this lecture of pure liquors, intoxicating liquors that are not adulterated, drugged, nor counterfeited; liquors that are what they purport to be, — pure, intoxicating liquors. Of these counterfeits we shall speak in another lecture.

Under the term "spirituous liquors," he "includes wine, porter, ale, beer, cider, and every other liquid which has undergone the vinous fermentation."

Now what is "vinous fermentation"?

When any sweet thing sours it is said to "ferment." Take any sweet liquid, put yeast into it, and let it "work," or "sour," and you have "fermentation."

If the liquid is kept tolerably cool — under 75 degrees of heat, it is called " vinous fermentation," because the liquid turns to "spirituous liquors." If the liquid is kept quite warm — over 75 degrees of heat, and under 90 degrees, it is called "acetic fermentations," because it turns to vinegar. So it depends upon the temperature, as to whether your sweet liquid, when it works, sours, or ferments, will turn to "spirituous liquor" or to "vinegar."

It often happens that it will first turn to spirituous liquor, and afterwards to vinegar;—owing to the fact that it is kept cool at first, but gets warmer afterwards.

Before your sweet liquid ferments there is no alcohol in it!

There is no alcohol in grape-juice before it ferments,—not a particle! There is no alcohol in apple-juice before it ferments,—not one atom! There is no alcohol in currant-juice, or any other sweet juice or sweet liquid, before it ferments,—not one single particle. These juices cannot make you drunk before they ferment! They cannot intoxicate before they ferment, because they contain no alcohol before they ferment. "Alcohol is the intoxicating ingredient." No sweet thing can intoxicate until after it "works" or ferments. Never! Alcohol is nowhere to be found, in all the fields of nature, until some sweet liquid has begun to ferment, or decay; for fermentation is a process of decay.

I quote again from the Dispensatory: "Alcohol is the product of sugar, in a liquid state, diluted, at a temperature of from 60 to 75 degrees, and the presence of a ferment called vinous fermentation."

There we have it: "Sugar in a liquid state, — diluted," that is, mixed with considerable water, or juice, and the presence of a ferment.

"Sugar will not undergo the vinous fermentation by itself; but requires to be dissolved in water, subjected to the influence of a ferment, and kept at a certain temperature."

Now what is a ferment?

"A ferment" means yeast, or, in Scripture language, 'leaven;' something that will make it rise, or blubber, or sour, or, what is better language, make it ferment.

This ferment has other names besides yeast and leaven. When put into bread, it is often called "emptyings" or "rising," and when put into vinegar, or other liquids, to cause them to "work," it is often called "mother," or "baum."

So that yeast, leaven, emptyings, rising, mother and baum, are almost synonymous terms, and mean about the same thing, — "a ferment."

A young lady, out in Arkansas, says, "It is the stuff what makes the doin's git up and confusticate!"

Many of the sweet liquid juices contain a ferment, already, within themselves, so that it does not become necessary to put one in. Such liquids will ferment or work of their own accord, if they are kept moderately warm and open to the air. All they want is just a little start, and they will work themselves. If kept cold and confined in air-tight casks, they will not ferment at all, — even if they do contain yeast. They will then remain as they are. But if kept warm, say between 60 and 75 degrees, and exposed to the air, they will undergo "vinous fermentation,"— or, what is the same thing, alcoholic fermentation. That is, the sugar in them, or the sweet principle in them, will be changed to alcohol, and they become "intoxicating liquors." But if they are kept still warmer, say from 75 to 90 degrees, and exposed to the air, they will undergo "acetic fermentation;" that is, the sugar in them will change into alcohol, and the alcohol will change immediately into acetic acid, which is the same as vinegar.

Sometimes merely shaking or jolting,

stirring, churning, or agitating the liquid, will cause it to begin "acetic fermentation," and change from alcoholic liquor to vinegar. As, for instance, you take a barrel of pure grape-juice, that has undergone the alcoholic fermentation, and you put it into a wagon, and jolt it over a rough road a few hours, or churn it, or shake it up thoroughly, and you will find, in a short time, it has undergone acetic fermentation or, what is the same thing, turned to vinegar.

The more sugar the more alcohol; or the more sugar the stronger the vinegar, as the case may be.

If, however, your liquid is very sweet, like syrup or molasses, having over thirty per cent. of its bulk pure sugar, and but little water, it will not ferment at all, at any temperature, whether it is kept warm, or cold, whether in air-tight casks, or exposed to the air; but will remain as it is, — syrup.

The pure juice of the best grapes contains about twenty per cent. sugar.

Now, if you put that juice into a kettle, and boil it down to one-half, it becomes a syrup, and will keep in any climate, — keep just as it is, — keep sweet, — keep fresh, — keep pure. And in this way you can always have on hand the pure sweet juice of the grape harmless as it comes from the cluster, and fresh from the hand of God. Because, when you have " boiled it down to one-half," you have simply evaporated one-half of its bulk, and evaporated nothing but water, leaving all the sugar and other nutritious substances in it. After it has been thus evaporated or "boiled down," about forty per cent. of what is left is pure sugar, and will keep in any land or latitude, in any climate, and for any number of years. And whenever you want a drink of the pure, sweet juice of the grape, you have only to add to the syrup its bulk in water, — just the same amount of water that you drove off when you boiled it down, — and you have it, pure as the fabled nectar of the gods, drawn from your heavenly Father's own brewery, — the vine-covered hills; and harmless as anything that nature produces on the broad lands of the earth!

When I travelled over the vine-growing countries of Europe, through Spain and France and Italy and Greece, I frequently purchased this kind of wine for my own use, and always when I could get it. And let me say right here, that with all the widespread drunkenness of Europe, — and it is absolutely awful to think about, — and with all the temptation that avarice offers to adulterate and poison and spoil the pure grape-juice of those sunny lands, still there are many temperate and intelligent men, who save for their own use, as well as to sell, a supply of the pure juice of the grape, as delicious as when it hung in the grape unpressed on the hill-adorning vine.

There are several other ways of preserving wine, besides boiling it down. You may can it the same as you can fruit. Put it hot into an air-tight can, and seal it. It will then keep just the same as canned peaches, or canned strawberries will keep, and just as long.

Still another way is to put it into barrels, or jugs, or bottles, and cork them up well, and sink them into a pool or stream of cold water. The ancients kept large quantities of wine in this way. The object is to keep the air and the warmth from it. And the barrels and jugs could be set into an ice-house. But perhaps the safest and easiest is to boil it down.

Anything that contains sugar can be kept in this way. The juice of the maple-tree, the juice of the sugar-cane, or sorghum, or beet, or apple or any other sweet thing, can be boiled down or canned, to preserve it.

So you see that the sugar, or syrup, or sweet principle — if you choose to call it by that name — must be " diluted " with water or juice, or liquid of some kind, before it will ferment.

" Alcohol," says the Dispensatory, — and I would have you mark the words, — " alcohol is the product of sugar, in a liquid state, diluted," etc.

Now, what kind of sugar? Any kind of sugar. Alcohol can be made of every kind of sugar, and out of every kind of juice that contains the sweet principle.

Out of grape-juice, apple-juice, cane-juice, peach-juice, pumpkin-juice, and water-mellon-juice. Beet spirit, or beet whiskey, is largely manufactured in France, from beet-juice.

A few one-ideaed temperance men have thought that the only way to bring about the reform, was to cut down the vineyards, and grub up the orchards, or refuse to plant them. What folly! What madness! Just about as foolish as the Shakers, who have come to the conclusion that the only way to destroy sin is to destroy the human race; and that they are going to destroy the human race by refusing to marry, live a life of celibacy, and just let the race run out!

You may dip the Mississippi river dry with a tin cup, you may batter the Rocky Mountains down with a knitting needle, or do any other "big thing" with very small tools, just as easy as you can destroy sin by the Shaker's plan, or do away with intemperance by "cutting down the orchards and grubbing up the vineyards." You cannot find fools enough to help you in the enterprise. There is no scarcity of fools, — not by any means. But that particular kind of a fool is a scarce article!

We have seen that alcohol does not exist in nature, anywhere, in all her vast dominions; but can be made by "fermenting" or souring any substance that contains the "sweet principle." Now, while we are on this part of the subject, let me ask, can you make it of anything that does not contain sugar?

And Chemistry shall answer the question. And again we quote from the United States Dispensatory: "One part of diastes mingled with two thousand parts of liquid

ITS NATURE AND EFFECTS. 23

starch, at a temperature of 160 degrees, will convert the starch into grape-sugar."

Aha! Starch can be turned into sugar with a little diastes! If you take two thousand pounds of starch, and wet it with water, so as to make a liquid, the same as it is when women use it to starch clothes with, and then put in one pound of diastes, and heat it all up to 160 degrees, you have converted the whole of the starch into sugar, — and grape-sugar at that! Then you will have in your hot water, two thousand pounds of grape-sugar made out of starch, and ready to boil down into syrup, and make into sugar, or else ready to ferment, until it turns into alcoholic liquor!

The United States Dispensatory, at page 446, says that "Malt consists of the seeds (of barley, rye, or corn), made to germinate by warmth and moisture, and then baked, so as to deprive them of vitality." Or, in other words, the barley is soaked in warm water until it sprouts, ready to grow, and it is then baked gently to keep it from growing any more.

The language of the Dispensatory is very scientific, and reminds me of the new way people have of saying "Root pig, or die!" The new way is "Perforate the particles of terra firma with your own proboscis, youthful porker, or else relinquish your vitality." He says, "The barley is made to germinate by warmth and moisture, and then baked so as to deprive it of vitality."

The reason it is soaked until it sprouts, is to enliven the diastes which is already in it, so that the diastes changes the starch into grape-sugar. And then it is baked, so as to keep it sugar, — so as to make it stay sugar.

Several other grains have diastes and starch in them, and will turn to sugar in the same way.

So, then, you can make alcohol out of everything that contains starch, by first changing the starch into sugar.

Now, what can you make starch out of? You can make starch out of corn. You can make starch out of wheat, and barley, and rye, and oats, and rice. You can make starch out of potatoes, and out of nearly everything that grows, that is good to eat. Starch enters largely into all the grains, many vegetables, and many fruits. And you can make alcohol liquor from all of them.

No use of "cutting down the orchards and grubbing up the vineyards," as long as we find the same thing, in a little different form, in all the grains, and in most of the vegetables and fruits of the whole earth.

You would have good time, "cutting down and grubbing up!"

Let us not think of such folly. Let us encourage the raising of grains and vegetables, and fruits of all kinds, including grapes and apples.

Plant your orchards and your vineyards, gentlemen. Raise your apples and your grapes. Cover the earth with trees and vines. Push on your productive industry with all your energy. March on with your enterprise, and let the earth bring forth abundance. Raise your fortunes from the earth. Let labor and land accumulate for your use and comfort, — a harvest of wealth.

But let us, at the same time, teach the people that it is not right to eat rotten grain, nor rotten vegetables, nor rotten grapes, nor rotten apples. There is plenty of these things that are not rotten.

Now, whoever drinks alcoholic liquors of any kind does just the same as if he were to eat rotten grains, or rotten fruits, because alcohol is a principle of death and decay, that is obtained from grains, and vegetables, and fruits, only after they have begun to ferment, decay, or rot, — all of which words mean about the same thing. In living and growing nature, alcohol can nowhere be found; but in dead and decaying nature we find it everywhere.

Decay is written upon all things. The flowers bloom and perish. The apple ripens, and falls, and rots. Set away the milk when it is warm, and it sours, moulds, and putrefies. You kill the ox, in a warm day, and the meat soon spoils, unless you take pains to preserve it. Man grows and perishes. As soon as life ceases decomposition begins.

The same principle prevails everywhere.

The juice of the fruit, unless boiled and canned, will very soon spoil; and when it is spoiling, we say it is rotting, or fermenting; for these words mean almost the same thing.

Imagine a citizen of Chicago eating "blue beef." You tell him, "Neighbor, you had better not eat that stuff." And he answers, "Why, you must be a fool to call this 'stuff.' Why, it's beef — it's ox-meat."

You say to him, "I know it is beef, — I know it is ox-meat; but then it is spoiled beef, — it is rotten ox-meat." But he replies, "What do you suppose I care if it is spoiled and rotten, — aint it beef? — aint it ox-meat? — and aint beef good to eat, — say?" You tell him, "It was good to eat once, but it is spoiled."

But he says, "I can't see the point. If it was good once, it is always good, and the older the better, and I'll down with it." So he chews away at the carrion, and thinks it is beef he is eating.

Some people shoot quails, and pigeons, and chickens, and let them hang out in the warm sun three or four days, just as they are, feathers, entrails, and all; and then, after the meat begins to get a little bit soft, they clean them and eat them. They call these "mulled" birds! I call it spoiled meat. People who like blue beef and mulled chicken, would naturally like decayed juice from rotten sugar, — which is alcoholic liquor.

When you find a decayed potato on your plate, you are not apt to eat it, because you know it is not healthy; and if you break a bad egg into your cup, you are not going to eat it, for the same reason. Then why should you drink decayed sugar and stagnant water?

If you take a gallon of beer and boil it half an hour, — long enough to evaporate the alcohol there is in it, — and then set it aside until it is cool, you would not begin to drink it. It would then be only a putrid mass of filthy slop. And fermented cider, the same. It will not take you long to try it. Boil fermented wine an hour, and afterwards try to drink it, and you will politely let it alone. Not any more of that kind, I thank you!

Dr. Henry Munroe, of Hull Medical College, England, says that "Alcohol is nowhere to be found in any product of nature, — was never itself created by God; but is essentially an artificial thing, prepared by man through the destructive process of fermentation."

It was for centuries supposed that alcohol was a simple chemical element, and that it could not be reduced or subdivided; but more recently it has been analyzed, and is found to be made up of

  4 parts carbon,
  6 " hydrogen, and
  2 " oxygen,

by measure. It is, in point of fact, a hydrated oxide of ethyl. Instead of being one simple element, it is a combination of three elements, in a definite and exact proportion. There are some foreign matters commonly mixed in with these three; one of which is fusil oil, of which I shall speak hereafter.

A dead horse lying out on the common, a dead cow in the back yard, or a dead dog in the ditch, exposed to the air, and exposed to the warmth, are converted into carrion and throw out a terrible stench or smell.

But did you know that a vat of rotting corn, or rotting rye or barley, or a cask of fermenting grape-juice or apple-juice, exposed to air and heat in the same way, are all undergoing the same process of decay or putrefaction that the dead carcasses are? The apple will rot; why not the juice? The grape will rot; why not the juice? Answer that if you can. Wet corn will rot. What is to hinder the juice of wet and sour corn from rotting?

They do rot, and in the same way that animal matter does, only they do not happen to have the same smell! So there is the difference, — and the only difference worth noticing — the difference of smell!

. All are decaying, all are rotting, all are fermenting, all are decomposing, all are putrefying alike; but the vegetables and fruits and juices do not happen to throw off quite the same stench that the carcasses of the dead animals do.

ITS NATURE AND EFFECTS. 33

Now, why the difference of smell? The answer is easy; and I will tell you.

The dead animals have nitrogen in their bodies, and that makes the stench. The putrefying grains and juices have no nitrogen in them, and hence they do not smell so badly. There is the difference.

Go into the brewery or distillery, and throw nitrogen into the vat of fermenting grain, or go down cellar where you have wine or cider fermenting, and throw nitrogen into them, and at once the terrible stench of putrefying carrion will be thrown off from your liquor. A little nitrogen will change the whole thing to carrion.

The nitrogen will not make them decay any faster, nor decompose in any different manner, but only makes the difference in the smell.

The decomposition and putrefaction of all animal matter, exposed to warmth and air, and the decomposition and putrefaction of all liquid vegetable matter, exposed in the same way to warmth and air, is the same, only in the one nitrogen is present, and in the other nitrogen is not present.

Since there is sugar in animal flesh, and since, in the process of decay, the sugar changes to alcohol, it follows that there is alcohol in carrion. And if it were nor for the nitrogen, which is also present, creating a strong odor, no doubt the distillers would be gathering up the old dead carcasses at the bone-yard, and distilling the juice out of them to sell to the topers! The alcohol, thus obtained, would be the same as any other alcohol. But the odor has heretofore been too strong an argument even for distillers.

Am I stating all this on my own authority, solely? — and the authority of Dr. Wood, author of the Dispensatory? — and the authority of Dr. Munroe, of Hull Medical College? You who think so will please turn to the Chemistry of Baron Von Liebig, one of the ablest chemists that the world has yet produced, and acknowledged as authority in the science of Chemistry everywhere. Turn to his book of Chemistry, and you will find these words: "Fermentation is nothing else but the putrefaction of a substance containing no nitrogen. Ferment or yeast is a substance in a state of putrefaction, the atoms of which are in continual motion."

There you have the words of the great German chemist, Baron Von Liebig, and higher authority in Chemistry cannot be found.

Let me repeat his words: "Fermentation is nothing else but the putrefaction of a substance containing no nitrogen."

While the vegetable lives, it reaches out

its roots and branches, and gathers food and nourishment from the earth and the air, and forms these into healthy compounds, by which its life and strength are built up. Fermentation or decomposition is the opposite of this, during which the life and strength of the vegetable or animal returns to the earth and air, scattering, tearing down, and dissolving strength.

Liebig says that "fermentation and putrefaction are stages of the return" of the nourishments of the vegetable to their original sources.

Life builds up; putrefaction tears down. Life gathers in strength; fermentation, or putrefaction, scatters and destroys that strength. "Life," says Liebig, "is opposed to putrefaction." And he further states that "alcohol cannot be evolved from the sugar of vegetable matter until after vinous fermentation sets in," which is the " death, or decomposition of vegetable matter." Thus Liebig authorizes all that I have said concerning fermentation.

Alcohol is, in fact, the death principle of the vegetable matter, out of which it is evolved; or the resulting principle of decomposition. It is found nowhere in living and growing nature; but everywhere in dying and dead nature.

And now you have before you the authority of one of the greatest chemists in the world, — and not disputed by any other responsible chemist, — Baron Von Liebig, of Germany.

Will the time ever come, when the German drinkers of beer and ale will listen to the learning and wisdom of their own immortal Liebig? Will the proud day of redemption from drunkenness ever come? Let us watch, and pray, and labor, while we patiently wait, and fondly hope for the coming of that day.

Again, if your liquid, after it has undergone vinous or alcoholic fermation, is found to contain twenty per cent., or more than twenty per cent., of alcohol, it will keep in any climate, at any temperature, and will not change to vinegar, even though exposed to warmth at 90 degrees or more, and exposed to the air; and even though you should shake it, and jolt it, and churn it about, it will remain as it is,—alcoholic or intoxicating liquor.

But if the intoxicating liquor contains less than twenty per cent. alcochol, it will not keep in all climates, but is liable to turn to vinegar at any time, either from the warmth of the liquor, or in moving it from place to place.

But the juice of the grape, after it has fermented, only contains twelve or fourteen, or at most but fifteen per cent. alcohol; and therefore cannot bear exposure to the summer weather, nor transportation from one place to another, without turning to vinegar.

Hence more alcohol has to be put into it, besides what it already has, so that it will have over twenty per cent. alcohol before it starts on its journey. This is a necessity, and cannot be avoided. Hence every gallon of the pure wine, shipped from a foreign country to this, or from one part of this country to another, has more alcohol added to it before it starts. All this foreign wine has put into it beet whiskey, or alcohol, or brandy (and hence called brandied wine), to make it stronger. And this, too, before it starts from its native hills.

And now the question arises, where do they get this extra alcohol, brandy, whiskey, etc., with which they strengthen the wines of commerce? And this question brings me to Distillation.

To answer it, we must know something about what is done at the distillery.

And here again, I quote from the United States Dispensatory: "Alcohol, being the product of vinous fermentation, necessarily exists in all vinous liquors, and may be obtained from them by distillation."

Or, in plainer language, there is alcohol in all fermented or decayed juices and liquids, and the way to get it out is to distil it out. Now, what is distillation? Let me tell you as plainly as I can.

If you take a kettle with any kind of liquid in it, and put it on the stove to boil, and then cover the kettle with a tight lid, leaving only one small hole in the lid for the steam to escape; and then take any kind of a long, hollow pipe or tube, and fasten one end of it over the hole in the lid, so as to make the steam run clear through the long, hollow tube before it can get out, and while it is going through be cooled and condensed, — and you have distillation.

If you put clear water in the kettle, and make the steam go over that way, through the pipe, and cool it, and catch it in a dish as it runs out of the pipe, the steam thus cooled and caught is called distilled water.

Now, if you put two liquids in the kettle together and boil them, the lighter one will turn to steam first, and will go through the pipe, get cool, and go out first; and the heavier one will stay in the kettle. For instance, if you put fermented grape-juice, — the same as fermented wine — into the kettle, and boil it, the alcohol that is in the juice, being the lightest, will go over through the pipe first, cooling as it goes, and be caught in a bucket at the other end of the pipe. What you have caught is only the steam of boiling, fermented grape-juice. That is all.

But that is brandy. The steam of boiling grape-juice that has been fermented or rotted is brandy! Hold your hands over a kettle of boiling wine — fermented wine, I mean — until the steam has wet them, and your hands are wet with brandy!

It is not a very mysterious process; not hard to learn. All you have to do is to boil the liquid, and catch the steam.

Now, what is there in the steam, as it goes over the pipe, or worm?

The alcohol, being the lighter liquid, starts over first, but it takes a little water along with it, and a little of the juice of the grape; and that is pure brandy. Alcohol, with a little water and a little grape-juice left in it, is pure brandy.

The bulk of the water, and all of the

grape-seeds, and skins, and dirt, and some of the other putrefying matter, stay in the kettle, and you can empty them out and throw them away.

So now you understand distilling. You merely heat up the liquid so as to make it into steam, and then drive the steam through a long pipe, which cools it, into a dish at the other end. That is all. And when you have distilled over all the best of your liquid, you can throw the rest away. The lighter one always goes over first, and the heavier one stays in the kettle.

You can distil fermented apple-juice in the same way, and then you have apple-brandy, or apple-whiskey.

You can distil fermented peach-juice in the same way, and then you have peach-brandy.

And so, from every fermented or rotted liquid that you can think of you can distil out the strongest of it, — the alcohol, — and throw the sediment away, or feed it to the hogs. Thus I have told you, in common language, how to distil. I shall try in all these lectures to use nothing but plain common language, that the people can all understand.

Sometimes they redistil the liquor; that is, after they have emptied the kettle, or boiler, they pour the liquor back in, and steam it through the pipe the second time. This time all the alcohol goes over, and only a little bit of the water; and the rest of the water is left in the kettle to throw away; and of course the liquor is stronger, because it has all its alcoholic strength, and less water. This is called rectifying. When you distil a liquor the second time, you rectify it. Sometimes they rectify a liquor two, three, or four times; and every time there is a little water left in the boiler to throw away; and of course the alcohol grows stronger or purer every time.

And now you know how to make alcohol. Take any fermented liquor, and distil it, and rectify it two or three times, and you have what is called pure alcohol.

It is not pure, however; because there is a little bit of water left in the very strongest alcohol, and also a little bit of fusil oil left in, that you cannot distil out, nor rectify out. So says the Dispensatory.

These distilling-kettles may be of any and all sizes, from a common coffee-pot up to a meeting-house; and you can distil from a quart a day, up to a thousand barrels a day.

Sometimes, when they rectify a liquor, they put other things in, to give it a new taste, that was not in it when it was fermented and distilled. For instance, they mix turpentine with distilled spirit, and then rectify it, and after that they call it common gin. That is the way gin is made. Distilled spirits, rectified with turpentine. That is what is the matter!

Did you know that when you were drinking pure gin, you were drinking a compound of decayed sugar, stagnant water, and turpentine.

Fellow-citizens, time will not allow me to complete this argument to night. It is necessary for us to be thorough in order that you may be entirely convinced. To-morrow night we shall close this investigation of alcoholic liquors, — their strength and composition, — present our authorities, and draw our conclusions.

WINE.

Let poets sing to the praise of wine,
In their sweetest tones and songs;

For the juice of the grape — from the Hand Divine —
    To the lips of the pure belongs.
But let them sing of wine that is new,
    Of wine that is not decayed,
Of wine that is fresh as the morning dew,
    From the stem in the arbor-shade.

But while they sing to the praise of wine,
    That is new, and pure, and sweet,
And tune their harps to the fruitful vine,
    And their carols of joy repeat,
Let them not forget that when decayed,
    Fermented or decomposed,
It has the great and brave betrayed,
    And their brightest prospects closed!

Let them not forget that a demon dire,
    Lies hid in fermented wine,
That will burn their health with a lurid fire,
    And hasten their life's decline;
That will fill the body with sores and pain,
    And cause them sorrow and woe;
And darken the mind with thoughts profane, —
    A fearful and dangerous foe!

Let them not forget that the hour of mirth,
    When fermented wine was used,
Has cast a shadow over the hearth,
    And the hearts of the loved ones bruised:

For the demon fierce, in the sparkling glass,
Is known by his deeds of yore;
He has mown his followers down like grass,
And he'll do as he's done before!

II.

The Nature of Alcohol — Where does it come from? — How can you get it? — How Much is there in the Liquor? — What is it good for? — And what is it?

(CONCLUDED.)

II.

As we stopped last night in the middle of our argument on the nature, strength, and sources of alcoholic liquors, let us complete the subject to-night.

And now, as you all fully understand what is meant by fermenting, and distilling, and rectifying, we are prepared to quote again, and quote largely from the United States Dispensatory : —

"Alcohol, being the product of vinous (or alcoholic) fermentation, necessarily exists in all vinous (or fermented liquors), and may be obtained from them by distillation.

"The distilled product of vinous (or fermented) liquors forms the different ardent spirit (or proof spirit) of commerce.

"When obtained (distilled) from (fermented) wine, it is called brandy.

"When obtained from fermented (cane) molasses, it is called rum.

"When obtained from fermented cider, it is called whiskey (or apple brandy).

"When obtained (distilled of course) from fermented malt-barley, it is called whiskey.

"When obtained from fermented rye, it is called whiskey (rye whiskey).

"When obtained from fermented corn, it is called whiskey (corn whiskey).

"When obtained from malted corn, fermented and distilled, it is called Bourbon whiskey.

"When obtained (distilled, remember) from fermented malted-barley, mixed with rye-meal and hops, and afterwards rectified with juniper berries (or seeds of the red cedar), it is called Holland gin.

"When obtained from fermented malted barley, mixed with rye-meal, or potatoes, and afterwards rectified from turpentine, it is called common gin.

"When obtained from fermented rice, it is called arrack."

Remember that I am still quoting from the United States Dispensatory, — an authority that none will deny.

"These (distilled) spirits are of different strengths, that is, contain different proportions of alcohol. Common proof spirits (or ardent spirits) are variable.

"Gin contains 51.60 per cent. of alcohol.

"Brandy contains 53.68 per cent. of alcohol.

"Rum contains 53.68 per cent. of alcohol.

"Irish whiskey contains 53.90 per cent. of alcohol.

"Scotch whiskey contains 54.32 per cent. of alcohol."

You will observe that this is a pretty full list of the principal distilled spirits of commerce, made and sold everywhere. More than half alcohol!

Dr. Wood has not given us the strength of arrack, nor beet spirit; but they are about the same as gin, — a little more than half alcohol; and diluted alcohol is half alcohol and half pure water.

Thus you have the relative alcoholic strength of all these spirits.

But although the strength of all these liquors is thus established by chemistry, they hardly ever — in fact — correspond with the standard thus fixed. Pure alcohol is the only one that you can depend upon at all. The rest of them are hardly ever what they pretend to be.

Dr. Wood tells the druggists and physicians not to use the common ardent spirits of commerce, because they are "so variable in their strength," and also "because of their impurities."

They have, as you have perhaps already noticed, four different names, all meaning about the same thing: Distilled Spirits, Rectified Spirits, Ardent Spirits, and Proof Spirits.

It matters little which of the four names you use, for they are all distilled, most of them rectified, all of them ardent, and all of them half, or a little more than half, alcohol; the remaining half being either water, or water mingled with other liquid substances, found in the various vegetables, fruits, and grains out of which they are all made.

All of them are made out of something that contains the sweet principle (sugar or saccharum), made to ferment, decompose, or, as Liebig has it putrefy, before they are distilled and rectified.

And here is perhaps the best place we shall find in this lecture to give a comparative table of the strength of all the various fermented liquors, from which all these ardent or proof spirits are distilled.

Some of these have their strength established by nature, when left as nature made them, and others are merely conventional. Those made from grains are merely conventional, because a bushel of malted barley-mash may ferment in five gallons of warm water, or ten gallons of warm water, of fifteen gallons of warm water, and will make the beer quite strong or weak, just as you desire; but those made of the juice or vegetables and fruits — if no water is poured into the juice, and none boiled away — are established by nature, and can vary only according to the kind and quality of the vegetables and fruits used.

Those that are made of grains are called Malt Liquors, or Grain Liquors, or Brewed Liquors.

Those that are made of juices or fruits are called Wines, or Fruit Liquors, or Native Juice Liquors

And both of these classes, collectively, have several names by which they are known in commerce.

They are called Fermented Liquors, Mild Alcoholic Liquors, Weak Alcoholic Liquors, Vinous Liquors, Undistilled Liquors, or Ancient Liquors.

It matters little by which of these names you call them, because they are all fermented only, and all contain a moderate proportion of alcohol, — and therefore vinous; but perhaps the first name given is the best, — Fermented Liquors, — because by this you can distinguish between them and the other class of liquors, that are made out of this class, that are first fermented and then distilled.

Beers, ales, and porters are made largely from barley and rye, but may be made from almost any kind of grain that contains starch.

The following table shows their strength when made according to the best approved rules, and unadulterated; and when not weakened by pouring water in, nor strengthened either by boiling water out, or pouring alcohol in, and before they are distilled.

THE STRENGTH OF FERMENTED LIQUORS.

Pale ale contains five per cent. of alcohol.
Common ale, six per cent. of alcohol.
Premium ale, seven per cent. of alcohol.
Small beer, five per cent. of alcohol.
Lager beer, six per cent. of alcohol.
Strong beer, seven per cent. of alcohol.

Porter, seven per cent. of alcohol.

Cider, six to seven per cent. of alcohol.

Rhubarb wine, seven to nine per cent. of alcohol.

Cherry wine, seven to nine per cent. of alcohol.

Strawberry wine, eight to ten per cent. of alcohol.

Currant wine, eight to ten per cent. of alcohol.

Raspberry wine, nine to eleven per cent. of alcohol.

Blackberry wine, nine to eleven per cent. of alcohol.

Peach wine, nine to eleven per cent. of alcohol.

Grape wine, twelve to fourteen per cent. of alcohol.

This list, although not complete, is sufficiently comprehensive to embrace most of the fermented liquors now in use. The grape wines are the strongest of them all, and afford the greatest variety.

Some of these grape wines are named after the cities and countries where they are supposed to be made; as Port wine, named after the city of Oporto, in Portugal; Madeira wine, named after the island of Madeira, where it is supposed to be made. French wines are made in France, — supposed to be, — and Spanish wines in Spain, etc. Others are named after the grape they are supposed to be made of; as, for instance, Catawba wine from the Catawba grape; Isabella wine, from the Isabella grape, etc. They are called Native wines, if made in this country, and Foreign wines if brought here from abroad.

I shall not take the trouble to give the fancy names to the various mixtures and compounds that are made out of the fermented liquors, and combined with distilled liquors. Their name is legion: Apple Jack, Black Strap, Ginger Wine, Bitters, and a host of others.

Some of these are very strong, and some of them are very weak.

It will be observed that none of these fermented, vinous, or ancient liquors contain as high as twenty per cent. alcohol; and therefore cannot bear exposure to the air, to warm weather, nor to transportation. To keep well, they must —

1st. Be kept air-tight.

2d. Be kept cool; and,

3d. Be kept still.

If any two of these three points are neglected, they soon spoil. Sometimes if one of these points is neglected, they will spoil. These liquors must be used up, soon after exposure, or they become worthless.

All these ciders and wines, or sweet

juices, could have been kept before they had fermented at all — and hence before there was any alcohol in them — just as well as now, —

1st. By boiling them down to one-half or one-third of their bulk.

2d. By heating and canning them.

3d. By sinking them in cold water, or setting them in an ice-house, where they would be constantly exposed to cold.

But now, since they have fermented, the only way to make them keep well, and at the same time expose them to warm weather and transportation, is to pour distilled spirit in upon them until the whole bulk shall be over twenty per cent. alcohol!

We hear people talk about "pure, unadulterated Port wine;" "pure, unadulterated Madeira wine," etc. Now, whenever those wines do happen to come over to us "pure and unadulterated," — which circumstance is very rare indeed, as I shall show in another lecture, — whenever they do happen to get here " pure," somehow or other they always happen to contain from twenty-one to twenty-three per cent. alcohol. Every time. Have never been known to fail. And the Distilled Spirit usually put into these " pure, unadulterated foreign wines," to inincrease their strength is beet whiskey or brandy.

But we are not blessed, however, with very many gallons of this kind of " pure, unadulterated foreign wine;" for when we think we are getting this kind, we almost always get a worse one, — drugged and adulterated, which I shall consider in another lecture.

I wish now to make an important remark about all these fermented liquors, — the whole class of them; and that is that their alcoholic strength is arranged on a sliding scale.

If they are boiled down one-fourth before they are allowed to ferment, it is plain that they will have the same amount of alcohol (from the same amount of sugar) in a less quantity of water; and therefore must be stronger. In this way their strength may vary, all the way from their own per cent. up to twenty per cent. alcohol.

They cannot go higher than twenty per cent., because, if they boil them too much, you make them into syrup, or fluid extract, and then they will not ferment at all.

The ancients never had any liquor stronger than twenty per cent. alcohol; because they cannot be made stronger than that, unless you distil them, or put distilled spirit into them.

And the ancients did not understand distilling. It is not quite six hundred years, since the process of distilling was first found out.

But in these days the dealer puts distilled or rectified spirits into them, just to suit his own taste and fancy, and to suit the taste and fancy of his customers.

You can buy wine which contains, —

  20 per cent. alcohol,
  or 25 " "
  or 30 " "
  or 35 " "
  or 40 " "
  or 45 " "
  or 50 " "
  or 55 " "

just to suit your notion!

And they will call it Port wine, or Madeira wine, or Sherry wine, or Champagne wine, or Portuguese wine, or Spanish wine, or French wine, just as you may desire.

And you can buy beer, and ale, and porter, and cider in the same way.

You pass a law that no license shall be

granted to sell ardent spirits or proof spirits; but grant them a license to sell beer only, and from that hour the drinker can get beer of any strength he desires. The dealer just simply pours distilled or rectified spirit or alcohol into his beer until his customer is satisfied. That is all. It is no trouble. Easily done. And then, besides, he knows his beer will keep. It won't spoil on his hands.

If you want beer that is ten per cent. alcohol, you say you will "take it square." If you want beer that is fifteen per cent. alcohol, you call for "good old beer." If you want beer with twenty per cent. alcohol, you call for beer "with a feather in it." If you want twenty-five per cent. alcohol, you call for beer "with a straw in it." If you want thirty per cent. alcohol, you call for beer "with a stick in it;" thirty-five per cent., beer "with a fly in it;" forty per cent., beer 'with a stone in it;" forty-five per cent., beer "with a broken back;" fifty per cent., beer "that is just a little bit lame;" fifty-five per cent., beer, which is stronger than old Scotch whiskey, you call for beer " with the devil in it!" And very well named, too. For in such beer as that you will find him — horns and all!

A gentlemen, the other day, saw his little daughter dipping her doll-baby's dress into a tin cup, and inquired, "What are you doing, my daughter?" "I'm coloring my doll's dress red, pa." "Coloring your doll's dress, red, — what with?" "With beer, pa!" "With beer! What put such a foolish notion into your head, child? You can't color red with beer." "Yes, I can, pa; because ma said it was beer that colored your nose so red!" And the gentleman had business that required him to be down town immediately.

So much is certain,— you can buy beer of any alcoholic strength that you may desire; and ale, and porter, and cider, and wine are sold in the same way. You hear such expressions as these, in all towns where license is granted to sell beer, or ale, or wine, or cider only: Beer, "sweetened with a maul and wedge!" Beer, "stirred up with a poker!" Beer, "with a black dog's paw it in it," etc.

They tell me that the greatest fit of laughter that the devil ever enjoyed, in all his life, and in which he nearly burst his satanic sides with excessive joy, was when he heard of a Temperance town that was so green and stupid as to grant a license to one of his imps to sell "wine and beer, only!" And they say that all his staff-officers joined in the laugh, and they giggled, and laughed, and haw-hawed, until all the hollow deeps of hell resounded with uproarious joy. So they tell me.

Beer only! Beer, "with a broken-back!" Beer, "sweetened with a maul and wedge!" Beer only! What foolish folly! What stupid stupidity! What nonsensical mockery!

But I intend to propose a plan, however, in one of these lectures, by which even that stupid plan can be carried out successfully.

A town that grants such a license as that, under present arrangements, soon finds itself in the same kind of a fix that the woman did who hated dogs. She wanted her husband to sell their old dog, or give him away, or kill him. She could not bear the sight of a dog. One night he came home, and said he, —

"Wife, I've sold that old dog!"

"Have you? Good, good! I'm awful glad of it! What did you get for him?"

"I got ten dollars."

"Did you? Good! I'm so glad you've sold him! Did you get your pay?"

"Yes, but not in money."

"Not in money! What did you get for pay?"

"I took it in pups, at two dollars a piece!"

So with a town that grants license for beer only. They have sold one dog, but they have got five instead!

Now, is alcohol good for anything? and, if so, what is it good for?

The United States Dispensatory says that "Alcohol is useful as a solvent." Solvent! What is a "solvent"? I will tell you as plainly as I can. Anything that will dissolve another thing is a solvent. For instance, water will dissolve sugar; therefore water is a solvent for sugar. Again, water will dissolve salt; therefore, again, water is a solvent for that article. Water is a solvent for many articles. But alcohol is also a solvent for many articles that water will not dissolve. For instance, alcohol will dissolve camphor, which water will not dissolve. Alcohol will dissolve a great many different articles. The Dispensatory says, "It is capable of dissolving a great number of substances; as for example, sulphur, phosphorus, iodine, ammonia, potassa, soda, lithia, the organic vegetable alkalies, urea, tannic acid, sugar, mannite, camphor, the resins, the balsams, the volatile oils, the soaps, and many other substances."

If you put wild-cherry bark into a kettle with a little water, and stew it, you will only get a little of the strength of the wild cherry. But if you put a little alcohol in, along with the water, you will immediately get all the strength of the wild cherry, and then you will have, —

1st. The strength of the wild cherry; and

2d. The water; and

3d. The alcohol; and

4th. The rough bark, which is worthless, all in the kettle together. But you need not keep them all together in that way. You can distil off the alcohol by itself, and keep it to use again. Then you can strain out the rough bark by itself, and throw it away. Then you will have left in the kettle only the water and the strength of the wild cherry. These you can boil down until it is very strong with the strength of the wild cherry, almost thick, like syrup, so that it will keep in any climate. Now, what is this wild cherry-juice, which you have boiled down until it is so thick and so strong? It is the fluid extract of wild cherry. And it will keep, without any alcohol in it, just as well as with it.

Molasses is the fluid extract of maple, and cane, and sorghum, and you know that molasses will keep without putting alcohol into it.

It is not necessary to make the tincture of maple, and the tincture of cane. They will keep as they are.

All the fluid extracts will keep as well as the tinctures.

But a great many roots, and herbs, and barks will not give up their strength, unless you, in this way, use alcohol as a solvent. But you can take the very same alcohol that you used in getting the strength out of the wild cherry, and put it into the kettle again, along with sarsaparilla roots and water, and get out all the strength of the sarsaparilla. Distil off the alcohol, by itself, and set it away, to use again. Then boil down the sarsaparilla juice until it is thick and strong, and you have the fluid extract of sarsaparilla, and you have the alcohol left yet.

There are hundreds of substances, very useful as medicines, that will not give up all their strength, unless you use alcohol as a solvent. So the Dispensatory is right, when it says, "Alcohol is useful as a solvent." But it does not take very much for that purpose; because, if you are careful to distil it all back every time you use it, you can use the very same alcohol forty different times, to get the strength out of forty different roots, barks, and herbs.

So we have learned that "alcohol is useful as a solvent;" and that we could not make medicine so fast, nor so successfully, without it. But we need not leave it in the medicine. We can distil it out every time, so as to leave the medicine by itself. Fluid extracts will keep in any climate, for a great number of years. And if you boil down the fluid extracts a little stronger, until they get thicker, you make them into solid extracts; the same as sugar, which is the solid extract of cane and maple; and currant-jelly, which is the solid extract of currants; or tar, which is the solid extract of pine.

No use of putting alcohol into medicines in order to make them "keep," as they will keep just as well without it, as with it. The United States Dispensatory, therefore, by which all the regular druggists, and regular chemists, and regular physicians are guided, recommends it as being "useful as a solvent" in making medicine.

The "American Dispensatory," written by Dr. John King, and by which all the eclectic and botanic physicians in the land are largely guided, says it is useful only as a solvent.

So does the "British Dispensatory," of England, and the "Dublin Dispensatory," of Ireland, by which books all the druggists, and all the chemists, and all the doctors are guided, in the whole British empire, throughout all her colonies. So does the French Dispensatory, which is standard authority with all the chemists, druggists, and physicians in the whole Empire of France. And so of the Dispensatories of Germany, Italy, and Russia. Open one of these dispensatories, and it says, "Useful as a solvent." Open another, and it says, "An excellent solvent." Open another, and it says, "Much valued as a solvent, in the preparation of medicines."

And I want to tell you something else, that these dispensatories say about alcohol. They all say it is poison!

The United States Dispensatory says, "It is a very powerful diffusible stimulant," and speaks of it as being a poison, which causes disease and death!"

The American Dispensatory says,." Undiluted, it is a. powerful irritant poison, rapidly causing intoxication, and in large quantities, death!"

The British Dispensatory says it is a poison.

The Dublin Dispensatory says it is a poison.

The French Dispensatory says it is a poison.

And all the Dispensatories that I have been able to examine say it is a poison.

Dungleson's Medical Dictionary says it is a poison.

Copeland's Medical Dictionary says it is a poison.

And I do not know of a respectable or

standard medical authority anywhere that does not class it among the poisons. Some of them call it a "narcotic poison;" some of them call it "an irritant poison;" some of them call it a "vegetable poison." But most of them agree that it is all three together,— a narcotic, irritant, vegetable poison: narcotic in its tendency, irritant in its action, and vegetable in its origin.

Professor Silliman, in his Chemistry, says "It is a powerful and dangerous stimulant."

Besides these Dispensatories and Medical Dictionaries — which are respected as authority everywhere — there are many prominent medical writers who class it as a poison, and who have given us the particulars of its poisonous effects.

Dr. Munroe, of England, says: "Alcohol is a powerful narcotic poison; and, if a large dose be taken, no antidote is known." And again he says: "A small quantity of pure alcohol, injected into the veins of an animal, has caused immediate death; showing alcohol to be a dangerous and deadly poison."

Dr. Elmer, of New York, says it is an "irritant, narcotic poison; and when taken into the stomach in large doses, no antidote is known."

Dr. Carpenter, author of Carpenter's Physiology, read by medical men everywhere, says it is a " dangerous poison."

Dr. Orfila, in his writings, says the same.

Dr. Pereira, in his writings, says the same.

So do Dr. Lees, and Dr. Christison, and Dr. Chambers, and Dr. Beck, and Dr. Taylor, and a host of others, and many of them among the ablest physicians now living.

Indeed, I do not know of a responsible

medical writer who dares to say it is not a poison.

I have quoted from dispensatories, and chemistries, and the medical dictionaries, and referred you to the standard medical writers of the age. Do you want higher auity? Higher authority cannot be found; more reliable books are not written.

Those who refuse to believe these authorities must be sceptical indeed, since they are in harmony with nature, which is the handwriting of the living God.

One more fact, and I shall close this investigation of the nature of alcohol; and that is, that nearly all of these authorities that I have been quoting say that "the best alcohol contains a little fusil oil," which is "a far more dangerous and deadly poison still." True, there is only "a little fusil oil" in the alcohol; but even that little is "dangerous and deadly."

ITS NATURE AND EFFECTS. 81

I shall not have time to quote from more than one authority on this point, and that one shall be the United States Dispensatory. And if any of you think I am not quoting correctly, just go to the drug-store and borrow the book (for it will cost you ten dollars to buy it), or to one of the physicians in town, who will be glad to lend it to you. Turn to the article on fusil oil, at page 77, and you will find these words: "This oil is always present in the products of alcoholic fermentation. It is an ingredient in the ardent spirit obtained from various grains, but is most abundant in that produced from fermented potatoes. In grain spirit it is present in the proportion of about one part in five hundred parts, by measure."

Various plans have been adopted to take the fusil oil out of liquors, and they have been partially successful. A large part of it is taken out by the process of rectifying, and more by filtering. But a little of it still remains, after they have done their best to take it out. It is never all taken out. Dr. Wood says, "The best alcohol contains fusil oil."

This oil is sometimes called grain oil, because found so largely in spirits made from rotted grain; sometimes called potato oil, because so abundant in spirits made from fermented potatoes; and is also and more properly called amylic alcohol, because it contains amyl, and in other respects has the same original ingredients with alcohol itself, though in different proportions.

"It is composed of

   10 parts carbon,
   12 " hydrogen, and
   2 " oxygen,

and is, in fact, a hydrated oxide of amyl.

As shown by experiments on inferior animals, it is an active, irritant poison."

It is a poison so deadly in its nature, that the doctors do not use it for any purpose. It was, at one time, used for lamp oil; but is now used chiefly by abandoned, heartless scoundrels, in adulterating liquors, and is not used by respectable men, nor for any honest purpose.

And now, fellow-citizens, what have we learned from these two lectures on the nature of alcohol?

We have learned that alcohol is the intoxicating ingredient in all pure intoxicating liquors, whether they are only fermented, or whether they are first fermented and afterwards distilled.

We have learned that alcohol is nowhere to be found in living and growing nature, throughout all her wide-spread fields, but only in dead and decaying nature.

We have learned that the sweet juices of fruits, before they are fermented, can do no harm, because they contain no alcohol; but are healthy and nutritious, — the best part of the fruit,— and are among the choice gifts that the All-wise Father has given to his children.

We have learned that alcohol is found in liquids, only after they have begun to ferment or decompose.

That fermentation is the same thing as decay, decomposition, and putrefaction.

That alcohol is the resulting death-principle of decaying nature, whenever it contains sugar in a liquid state.

That the reason why rotting vegetable matters do not have the same smell as other carrion is because they do not happen to contain nitrogen.

That all substances that contain sugar may be converted into alcohol by this process of decay; but that they can be kept from decay, pure, sweet, and healthy, by using a little care in boiling, canning, and sealing them up from the air.

That all grains, and fruits, and vegetables, that contain starch, may have the starch converted into sugar by diastes, and then converted into alcohol by fermentation or putrefaction; and therefore the utter folly of trying to discourage the raising of orchards and vineyards.

That the alcoholic strength of all undistilled intoxicating liquors is arranged on a sliding scale, so that beer, ale, porter, cider, and wine can be made to contain any per cent. of alcohol desired.

That undistilled intoxicants have not sufficient alcoholic strength to stand exposure to the air, heat, and transportation, unless additional alcoholic strength is given them so as to raise it to at least twenty per cent.

That this is done by pouring into them distilled or rectified spirits or alcohol.

That none of the wines of commerce — not even the best — contain less than twenty or twenty-one per cent. alcohol.

That the alcoholic strength of ardent or distilled spirits, although established, is hardly ever adhered to.

That alcohol is itself a narcotic and irritant poison.

That the best of alcohol contains fusil oil, — a still more deadly poison.

That alcohol is useful in the preparation of medicine as a solvent only.

And that we have learned these facts from the highest written or printed authorities on the whole earth, — the standard works of chemistry and medicine, adopted by the wisest nations.

All these tell us that alcohol is poison. And many a victim to its wiles, fallen prematurely by its terrible effects, has reached out a nervous hand to his mourning friends, and whispered sadly, with his last farewell to earth, in broken accents, "Poison! poison!"

HOW THE VICTIMS DIE.

Shun, oh, shun the poison cup !
Shun, oh, shun fermented wine !
It burns the soul of manhood up,
And mars the human form divine.
Greet not the envenomed monster. No !
Greet not the fiend who lures to kill ;
He lays his fond admirers low ;
They sleep in every vale and hill.

Avoid the dens where wine is sold ;
Avoid the path that drunkards tread ;
These places make the youthful old,
And lay them, early, with the dead.
Resist the charms they fain would throw
Around the mocker, with a lie ;
Resist the charms ; for those who go
Within his magic circle, die.

They die in want, they die in pain,
And woes no tongue has power to tell ;

Bereft of friends, their honor slain,
   Within the prison's gloomy cell.
Their comrades laugh to see them fall,
   And laugh to see them die alone,
Exposed, beside some ruined wall,
   Their death-bed hard and chilly stone.

They started on life's happy morn,
   As proudly forth as you or I,
With souls as great, as nobly born,
   With loves as fond, and hopes as high;
But few will care, in kindness now,
   Since drink has darkened them in gloom,
To wipe the death-damp from their brow,
   Or plant a flower upon their tomb.

III.

ALCOHOL — WHAT EFFECT HAS IT UPON THE HUMAN BODY? — DOES IT EVER CAUSE DISEASE AND DEATH? — WHAT PART OF THE SYSTEM DOES IT INJURE? — HOW AND WHY?

III.

CHEMISTRY has analyzed everything that men use for food; and it has found out exactly what food is made of. Chemistry has also analyzed the human body itself, so as to ascertain what is needed to supply any injury or waste. It is found that the body needs and requires just what the food contains.

Now, what does the body need; and what does the food contain?

I quote from Dr. Munroe, who says, "Every kind of substance employed by man as food, consists of sugar, starch, oil, and glutinous matters, and the glutinous matters are composed of fibrine, albumen, and caseine."

Alcohol does not seem to be in the list,

and therefore cannot be food. Fruits and grains contain these substances, and so do the fresh juices; but all these substances must first decay before alcohol is obtained from the fruits and grains. Alcohol is evolved, not from food, but from decayed food. Alcohol contains none of these substances, and therefore cannot be food.

"There is more food in one bushel of barley, than there is in 12,000 gallons of the best beer." So says Baron Von Liebig.

But alcohol is not food, for several other reasons. All food, when taken into the human stomach, is digested, and transformed into something that will renew and build up the body. When we eat bread and meat and potatoes they are digested and help to supply the wear and tear and waste that are constantly going on, and give new strength to the body. Some of the food goes to build up the bone, some to make muscle, some to supply heat, some to make nerve and brain, and some to supply the various juices of the system. But alcohol does none of these things, and therefore cannot be food. It passes out of the body, just as it goes in, unchanged, undigested alcohol!

And now let us see if we can find out the reason of this fact.

If you dip a feather into pure alcohol, and then open your eye, and lay the feather flat on your eyeball, how quick it will smart and burn, and how quick you will have to take it off again! The eye, with all its lids and coverings that the alcohol has touched, then tingles and smarts, and becomes red and bloodshot, and swells, and the tears commence running, and the eye tries in every way to drive out the alcohol! Three or four such applications will make you have sore eyes for several days; and you will not have to repeat the operation many times to destroy the eyesight altogether. Now, why? Because the alcohol irritates, burns, and poisons the tender coatings of the eye. It is an irritant, burning poison.

Again: If you fill your mouth full of alcohol, and try to hold it there, the lining of your mouth begins to burn and smart, and pain you, so that you will very soon have to spit it out. Examine your mouth then, and you will find it very red and bloodshot or, what is the same thing as bloodshot, the small veins of the mouth are congested, or filled full of blood, and the whole lining of the mouth is inflamed and a little sore. And why? Because the tender inside of the mouth is irritated and scorched and poisoned by the alcohol. That is the reason.

Fill your eyes with pure water, and it

will not make them smart, nor inflame them. Swimmers open their eyes in the water when they swim, both in fresh and salt water, and they are not harmed. Fill your mouth with water, and it will not be burned, nor will its veins be congested with blood.

Lay a piece of nice clean beef-steak on your eyeball, and let it lay there, and it will not inflame the eye. If it should happen to be already inflamed and sore, the beef-steak will feel cool and soothing to it; and even if the beef should happen to be a little salty, no injury will follow. Fill your mouth with beef-steak, and it is not going to hurt you! Put a bread-and-milk poultice right into your open eye, and let it stay there all night, and your eye is not injured! Many do that to cure sore eyes. Put a large bread-and-milk poultice into your mouth, and it will not poison you! I have tried it, and recommend it as a pleasant experiment!

I have made these comparisons to show the difference between the action of an irritant, or poison, on the tender membranes of the body, and the action of food on those same tender membranes.

But the lining membranes of the stomach and bowels and all the inside works of the human body are tender and easily injured, the same as the coatings of the eye and the linings of the mouth.

These coatings and linings are all of the same material, and whatever irritates and injures one, will irritate and injure them all.

Hence, whenever alcohol touches the interior parts of the human system, it irritates and burns and congests and inflames them, and makes them very active to throw off or get rid of the intruder! Or, in other words, it stimulates them to unnatural activity,—makes them active in trying to get rid of the poison,—alcohol!

Why should we fill our stomachs with a poison liquid which is strong enough to "dissolve sulphur, and dissolve iodine, and dissolve ammonia, and dissolve potash, and dissolve camphor, and dissolve resin, and dissolve all the organic vegetable alkalies?" What is the use of it? As well drink nitric acid, or sulphuric acid, or chloroform, or the oil of vitriol, or kerosene, or any other deadly poison. For God made one just as much as he did the other. There is nothing in the normal nature of man that calls for any of these poisons.

The United States Dispensatory says this irritating poison "is a very powerful diffusible stimulant." Anything that increases the activity is a stimulant. Anything that stimulates the nerves and brain is a narcotic stimulant. Anything that stimulates the heart and arteries is an arterial stimulant. But this is a "diffusible stimulant." That is, it diffuses itself everywhere, through the whole body, and stimulates every part that it touches.

It would be just as correct to say that it irritates every part that it touches, for it is an irritating stimulant.

I do not know that I can better illustrate what is meant by a "very powerful diffusible stimulant" than by supposing a case.

Suppose that fifty men were standing in a row, just a few feet apart, passing cannonballs to each other. One takes up the iron ball, tosses it to the next, who catches and tosses it to the next, and so on, until it passes down to the other end of the line, and is thrown down. And then another ball is passed down, and another and another, and all the men work easily, deliberately, and steadily as the balls are passing. But pretty soon the second man cries out, "Hot ball! burning my hands! take it, quick!" And the next one catches it, and calls out, "Hot ball! Here! Hot ball!" And the next one that gets it instantly yells out, "Hot ball! Make haste!" And so on, all the way down the line, each one is in haste to get rid of it, and says, "Confound the ball!" "Scorching hot!" "Blistering my hands!" "What is the use of sending hot ones?" "Take it!" "Hurry!" But before they have time to cool their hands or heal them, down comes another ball, hotter than ever, and one screams out, "It's burning hot! Take it!" And the next, "For God's sake, take it!" And the next, "Hotter than ever, hyer!" And another, "My hands are blistered, hyer!" And still another, "Can't hold it, hyer!"

One man along down the line, calls out, "Tell that first man not to send any more hot balls!" And others say, "He's deaf! He's deaf! He cannot hear us!" "We'll motion to him," screams another. "He's blind! He's blind! He cannot see us motion!" "He is picking up hot balls with glass gloves. He does not feel their heat!" "We shall have to take them as they come!" And while they are yet talking, down comes another, seething, fiery hot, and the men with seared and blistered hands take them and pass them on, hot as they come.

But you say, "Why don't the men drop the hot balls, as a dog does a hot potato?" Ah, but they cannot drop them. A man may now and then "drop" one of them into his bosom, or into his pocket, or lay it on his foot; but it will burn a sore wherever it stops.

ITS NATURE AND EFFECTS. 101

Once the alcohol having passed into the mouth, and down the throat, it has to pass on down the whole line; or if it stops it burns a sore. The hand passes it into the mouth, and into the stomach it goes. The stomach calls out "Hot ball!" and throws it, as quick as possible, into the blood. The blood says, "Hot ball take it!" and swiftly throws it into the heart. The heart pumps it into the arteries, and the arteries rush it into the brain, and skin, and everywhere, trying to drive it out. The pores of the skin open, and say, "Throw it out here!" The lungs open, and hurl some of it off with the breath. The liver takes a part of it, and the kidneys take some of it, and pass it through the urine. The whole system makes haste to get rid of it, and does get rid of it. It is thrown out of the system just as it went in, — undigested, — unchanged, — alcohol. But part of it remains in the system, — lodges in the various organs of the body. What about that part? Further on I will tell you.

We have now learned what is meant by a "diffusible stimulant." Something that stimulates to unnatural activity everything it touches. And " alcohol is a very powerful diffusible stimulant," and an "irritant narcotic poison."

But perhaps you think I am stating this on my own authority solely. Not entirely so. I shall quote a few authorities.

Dr. Henry Munroe, who is a professor and lecturer in a medical college, at the city of Hull, in England, says, "Alcohol, whether taken in large or small doses, immediately disturbs the functions of the body and the mind." And again he says, " The only influence of alcohol on the stomach is that of an irritant."

There it is in a few words. It irritates

the stomach. That is what it does to it,— irritates it. And if you were to call it an irritant, instead of a stimulant, it would be just as well named.

Dr. Munroe also says, "As soon as the alcohol has been absorbed into the blood it is carried by the tide to the heart, the inner surface of which organ, disturbed by the presence of the alcohol, pumps away so much the faster to get rid of the intruder." To get rid of what? "The intruder." Ah, it is not food, then, but only an intruder!

Dr. T. K. Chambers, who is physician to the Prince of Wales, the heir-apparent to the throne of England,— and therefore supposed to be the first-class physician, says, "It is clear that we must cease to regard alcohol as, in any sense, an aliment (a food), inasmuch as it goes out (of the body) as it goes in."

Ah! It does not change into bone. It

does not help to build up muscle, nor nerve, nor brain, nor any of the juices. But simply an irritant which goes plunging through the body, singeing and burning till it gets out, like the hot balls passed along the line of men. Let me quote from the United States Dispensatory: —

"In a diluted state, alcohol excites the system, renders the pulse full, and gives additional energy to the muscles, and temporary exaltation to the mental faculties. As an article of daily use, alcoholic liquors produce the most deplorable consequences. Besides the moral degradation which they cause, their habitual use gives rise to dyspepsia, hypochondriasis, visceral obstructions, dropsy, paralysis, and not unfrequently mania.

"Its effects as a poison. When taken in large quantities, alcohol, in the various forms of ardent spirit (or proof spirit), produces a true apoplectic state, and occasionally speedy death."

Here you have Dr. Wood: "In a diluted state, it produces the most deplorable consequences. Moral degradation!" and a number of terrible diseases of the body.

Dr. Rudolph Masing, one of the ablest physicians of Germany, has prepared a new test for alcohol. It is this: —

"Just put a solution of bichromate of potash and sulphuric acid into a glass tube, leaving one end of the tube open. The color of this solution is red; but a very little alcohol will turn it to emerald green. Sober men breathed into it, but their breath had no effect. A drunken man breathed into it, and it instantly turned green. Young ladies should have this test-tube filled and ready, and let their lovers breathe into it. If the test-liquid turns green, tell him that you cannot appreciate his color. Make him wait till he ripens.

But what does this test prove? It proves there is alcohol in the drunkard's breath. And what does that prove? It proves that alcohol goes out of the body just as it goes in, — without changing or digesting; and, therefore, cannot be food, nor can it aid in building up or renewing any part of the body. It is still alcohol.

Dr. Lallemand, of France, and Dr. Perrin, of France, both of whom stand at the head of their profession in that great empire, assisted by the great French chemist, Duroy, have been trying many experiments by the same chemical test.

A man, who drank a pint and a half of wine at half past ten o'clock, breathed into the test-solution at noon, and it turned green in two minutes. The same at one o'clock. At two o'clock it turned green in four minutes. At five o'clock it turned green in fifteen minutes. At six o'clock it made but a slight change. At seven o'clock no change at all.

Dr. Magendie, more than fifty years ago, and Dr. McNish, and others, by the aid of other tests, proved that alcohol passed out of the system from the lungs and pores as it went in; and they proclaimed that fact to the world. Now it is proved beyond a doubt. Therefore no part of it is food, but only an irritant, scorcher, poisoner,—a thing that inflames whatever part it touches while rushing through the body, and causes terrible ulcers and putrefying sores wherever it stops.

By the same tests, also, these gentlemen find that alcohol passes out through the skin. They made a dog drink whiskey,— remember they had to *make* him do it against his will, because he knew better than to drink of his own free will,—and, after he was drunk some hours, the perspiration from his skin turned the test-liquid green. Thus nature throws off the biggest part of the alcohol that is taken in at the stomach. But, alas! it is not all thrown off. Some of it finds a lodgment and remains, causing the drunkard pain and sorrow.

These gentlemen next examine the urine of the drunkard, and find alcohol there. Then they cut open dead drunkards, and find alcohol in the blood, alcohol in the heart, alcohol in the liver, alcohol in the kidneys, alcohol in the bowels, and alcohol in the brain.

They found it everywhere in the system, causing sores and diseases; but the liver suffered the most from it, and the brain next; the kidneys and blood next. And, what is more, they found the stomach and other organs where the alcohol was and had been, irritated, congested, inflamed, sore, burned, charred, ulcerated, and diseased, by the "irritant, narcotic poison." They found that those who drank the most were injured the most; but those who had only drank moderately of beer, ale, or wine, all injured, in proportion to the amount of alcohol they had consumed.

Now, what do you think of alcohol? No wonder the drunken sot has a fiery red nose. No wonder his eyes are bleared and bloodshot. No wonder his face is bloated and his arm trembles. He is literally burned out! And what there is left of him is only the ulcerated and diseased form of what might have been a man.

Let me quote a little more testimony on this point, from the United States Dispensatory. I like to quote from these solid old authors, because the people are going to believe them. The article I quote was written many years ago, by the wise old Dr. George B. Wood. "After death, abundant evidence is furnished of the absorption of the alcohol" (into the system). By Dr. Percy it has been detected in the brain; by others, in the ventricles (of the heart), and by Dr. Wright, in the urine. There is testimony that has never been disputed. And here is more. A man fell suddenly dead in the streets of London, and was carried into Westminster Hospital and dissected. And the doctors found a quantity of "limpid fluid" pushed in upon the brain; and this limpid fluid was found to be one-third gin. They smelt it, and tasted it, and then lit a match and burnt it. It was gin, which is more than half pure alcohol.

Thus the remains of the dead record the history, character, and habits of the soul that filled them. The biography of the man is written on the organs of his body, in burning and eternal letters, by every act of his daily life; and the follies and vices of the drunkard are stamped in his silent ashes.

But there are those who suppose that, although aclohol is not food, still, in some way or other, " it aids digestion and is good for the stomach." This is again a mistake. The reverse is true. It prevents the digestion of food, and thus brings disease upon the body.

Let me prove this proposition to you. Dr. Figg, of Scotland, had two healthy dogs of the same size. He cut up four ounces of cold roast mutton into square chunks for each of them. He gave them the meat at the same time. He then forced an ounce and a half of distilled spirit down the throat of one of the dogs only. After three hours he killed both dogs. The dog that drank the ardent spirits had the meat left in his stomach just as it was when he ate it — undigested. But the other dog's stomach was empty, — the meat having been all properly digested. It prevented digestion in the dog's stomach. Why not in the human's?

Let me give you another experiment now, — this time a human experiment.

The laborers in a shop near Edinburgh were paid off on Saturday, just after dinner. They rushed into the saloons near by, and got drunk. They stayed drunk, and ate nothing until noon the next day, when their money gave out. Then, when they were beginning to get sober, they had the headache and felt sick at the stomach, and sent for Dr. Figg. He gave them each an emetic, to make them "heave up Jonah." In a few moments they did heave up Jonah;

but Jonah was their Saturday's dinner. Alcohol helped their digestion with a vengeance. Healthy food in a healthy stomach will digest in two or three hours. Their dinners did not digest in twenty-six hours. Why? Because the alcohol in the liquor they drank prevented digestion. That was the reason why.

Once more. I had a patient once, who ate some cucumbers and onions along with his dinner. He then went off and got on a " bender," and kept drunk for two days, eating nothing. He became sick as well as drunk, with severe pains in his stomach, and sent for me to come and sober him up. I gave him a vomit, and in a few minutes the cucumbers and onions paid us a visit. They had been forty-eight hours digesting, and then did not digest. Why? Because liquor prevented digestion, and made the man sick. You have seen instances of this kind yourselves, and if you will take a second thought, you will all of you know that it does not aid, cannot aid digestion, but it directly prevents digestion, and is therefore an injury to health.

Good medicine is sometimes put into liquor, which may to some extent counteract the evil effects of the liquor; but how much better it would be to take the medicine by itself, and leave the liquor alone! Hops by themselves are a tonic, and a useful medicine. Malt, by itself, is chiefly sugar, and therefore useful as food. But when they are "soaked in warm water, and allowed to rot," they cease to be food entirely, and lose nearly all their tonic effect, and become a mild alcoholic liquor, which is injurious.

Some people, who think they are very smart, will go and take a glass of beer, ale, porter, wine, or brandy, "just to assist digestion." If they knew one-fourth part as much as they suppose they do, they would know that these liquors prevent digestion, just in proportion to the amount of alcohol they contain.

Dr. Sewell says, "Man, by nature, has no taste nor desire for alcohol; it is as unnatural and averse to his constitution as it is to the horse or the ox; and there is no apology for its use by man that does not equally apply to the brute."

And Dr. Sewell is right. Every word of that quotation is true, and cannot be disproved.

Now, let me give you a little, slight touch of the science of physiology and chemistry.

When you eat, there is a juice comes into your mouth, from the glands of the mouth, called saliva. When you have swallowed the food into the stomach, there is another juice flows in from other glands, called gastric juice. When the food starts into the bowels, still another juice flows in, called pancreatic juice. These three juices all combine together and completely digest or solve the food. It requires about one quart of these juices every day for digestion. They are solvents, and will dissolve the food you eat. If you analyze these juices, you will find that the strong solvent principle in all of them is pepsin. So that pepsin is what dissolves and digests the meat and bread, and all the food you eat, of whatever kind. You cannot digest any food unless you have plenty of pepsin in the stomach. Pepsin is a powerful solvent. But so is alcohol a powerful solvent.

Now, suppose the two solvents get into the stomach together. What will be the consequence? The consequence is, the two solvents are bound to fight. "When Greek meets Greek then comes the tug of war." One solvent is going to dissolve the other solvent. One of the two solvents has to perish. Which one will perish? Which will be victorious, and kill the other?

I will tell you: Alcohol dissolves pepsin, and therefore stops digestion in an instant of time. And as a consequence, digestion cannot go on so long as alcohol remains in the stomach.

When the alcohol is driven out of the stomach, and new pepsin comes in, then digestion can go on, and not till then. You may talk about "beer to promote digestion," and "ale to assist digestion," and "wine to help digestion," until old age overtakes you; but there stands a scientific fact, which you can neither alter nor remove, — alcohol dissolves pepsin. There it stands, — a scientific principle, — a scientific fact.

That principle, or scientific fact, is deduced from the eternal laws of nature, of which God is the author; and while God and his works remain, that fact will remain unchanged.

Viewed in the light of science, does it not look supremely ridiculous for a man of common, ordinary intellect to talk about drinking alcoholic liquor to "assist digestion"? If you happen to meet such a man in your travels, just please to ask him for me, if you please, quietly, if it would not be a profitable transaction for him, to sell whatever he may possess of this world's goods, and buy a gimlet, in order that he may have a small hole bored in his head so as to let the simples out? They used to bore for the hollow-horn; he should, by all means, be bored for the simples.

But seriously, this thing of drinking "for digestion" has become so common, that it is time for somebody to speak the truth upon the subject boldly. The truths of chemistry, when once discovered, are everlasting. The science of chemistry has become a mighty power in this land of learning; and who knows but it will yet solve the knotty riddle of drunkenness, and work out the great problem of the temperance reform?

"Ah, but, Dr. Story, hold a moment! You are giving all this about pepsin on your own sole authority, are you not?"

Not entirely so. I am happy to say that I am backed up by the highest authorities, and these statements proved by a multitude of experiments. I will mention a few.

Dr. Munroe, of the Hull Medical School, has made a number of experiments, of which I shall mention one. He mixed some bread and meat in a vial along with some gastric juice. He then corked the vial up, and set it in a little box of warm sand, and kept it about as warm as the healthy stomach would be, and occasionally shook the box, so as to imitate the motion of the stomach. He also fixed another vial, in the same way, only in the second vial he put a little pale ale along with the bread and meat and gastric juice.

In the first vial, the food was digested in from six to eight hours. But in the second vial, which contained the ale, the food would not dissolve at all, though he kept it warm for several days. Why? Because the alcohol in the ale dissolved the pepsin in the gastric juice, and prevented digestion.

My second authority is Dr. Dundas Thompson, who says that "alcohol when added to the digestive fluid (the juices just named) produces a white precipitate, so that the fluid is no longer capable of digesting food."

Dr. Todd and Dr. Bowman say that "the use of alcoholic stimulants retards digestion by coagulating the pepsin, — an essential element of the gastric juice,—and thereby interfering with its action."

Dr. Figg says that "if a man after dinner, drinks two or three glasses of spirits, the gastric juice in the stomach will be neutralized."

I have now given you the names of seventeen prominent medical writers, all of whom base their knowledge on actual experience.

One more authority on this point, and then I shall take up another division of the subject. And this time a high American authority,—Dr. Thomas Sewell, of Columbia Medical College, of Washington City, who has been a prominent medical man before the country for nearly half a century, as a practical physician and teacher of pathology and medicine. He says, "There are some substances upon which the gastric juice has no action, or, if any, it has not the power of converting them into nutriment; and alcohol is one of them."

Now you have authority — and good authority, — besides the authority of Dr. Story. And all these authorities go to show that alcohol never helps digestion but always hinders, retards, and prevents digestion. They show that no amount of it, however small or however great, can assist digestion, but must always injure it.

They show that a glass of pale ale or small beer, containing only five per cent. alcohol, and a glass of Scotch whiskey, which contains fifty-four per cent. alcohol, have exactly the same effect upon the human system, in proportion to their alcoholic strength.

Anything that retards or prevents digestion must injure the whole body, because indigestion is itself the prolific cause of many diseases. Food ought not to lie in the stomach undigested, for so many hours and days.

Dr. Sewell says: "Digestion is one of the most important of all the animal economy, indeed it is indispensable to the due performance of all the other functions; consequently when this becomes impaired the whole system languishes, and all the other functions become, sooner or later, affected also." Besides this, the great waste of the juices containing pepsin will bring on diseases. During one day a healthy set of glands furnish the stomach with nearly a quart of juice. Now, if you drink a few glasses of liquor and destroy that juice, then the glands must furnish more. When you destroy that with still more drink, they furnish still more of it. But by and by, the glands being overtaxed, become exhausted and fail to supply the necessary juice. Then chronic indigestion, and other diseases, and death must follow.

And now I am ready to speak of the various diseases of the body, caused by the habitual use of alcohol. And I propose to get right down to the work. In this division of the subject I propose to show you some things in the way of alcoholic diseases, compared with which, all that have been noticed heretofore are but toys and playthings.

And first, of the stomach.

More than fifty years ago, there was a surgeon in the United States army, who made a great many examinations into a living stomach. It happened in this way. A stout, healthy boy, about eighteen years of age, by the name of Alexis St. Martin, a Canadian, was shot in the stomach with a shot-gun. The discharge tore quite a large hole clear through into the stomach, so as to let all the food fall out in front. Dr.

Beaumont dressed the wound, and it finally healed up. But when it healed up, it left a hole clear through, about an inch in diameter. This hole had to be plugged up, or corked up, with a silver cork, or plug, so as to keep the food in his stomach when he eat. To keep this plug in its place, the boy had to always wear a belt around his chest. The boy got well and lived a great many years, but always had to wear the belt and silver plug. Whenever you wanted to look into the inside of the stomach, all you had to do was to get him to lie down on his back, and slip the belt down a little, and take the plug out, and just look right in, and see his bread and dinner. Wouldn't it be handy, if we all had just such a little hole in our stomachs? so that whenever we eat too much, we could reach right in with our thumb and finger, and claw out a part of it. Some of us would have to hire an active man to take it out half as fast as we put it in.

Dr. Beaumont used to look into the young man's stomach every day; and continued to do so for more than fourteen years.

And the doctor hired the young man to go with him to Washington City, and to stay with him there, on purpose to try experiments with food and drink in his stomach. The inside of a healthy stomach has a light-pink color, as all doctors well know.

(*See Sewell's Plates, No.* 1.)

And as Alexis St. Martin was a healthy, stout boy, his stomach was pink-colored also, at first. But by and by he got so he liked liquor; and, as he had grown to be a man, the doctor had to let him do as he pleased. After he had been drinking pretty hard for a few days, Dr. Beaumont looked into his stomach, and found it — no longer pink, but fiery red, and very much congested or inflamed. When St. Martin would quit drinking for a few days, the doctor would look in, and find the stomach pink-colored, healthy, and all right again.

Dr. Beaumont wrote a book all about it long ago, before the Temperance Reform began. Out of that book I make this quotation : —

"The free use of ardent spirits, wine, beer, or any of the intoxicating liquors, when continued for some days, has invariably produced those morbid changes in St. Martin's stomach."

Ah! invariably done it. And the doctor made these kind of examinations for fourteen years. Well, that is something; but I have something more. Dr. Thomas Sewell, who was then a young doctor, used to go and look into St. Martin's stomach sometimes along with Dr. Beaumont. Afterwards Dr. Sewell got into a big practice, and got to be President of Columbia College at Washington City. Sometimes men would die drunk, or get killed while they were drunk, and Dr. Sewell would have them carried up into his college, and he would cut them open, and look into their stomachs and bowels and livers and hearts. And as time rolled on, Dr. Sewell kept on dissecting and looking into drunkards' stomachs, and examining all their insides, until he has spent more than forty years, and looked into the inside works of more than three hundred drunkards. And what does he say? He has published a book, giving an account of alcoholic diseases; and I shall quote.

He says that in the "stomach of the temperate drinker,— the man who takes his grog daily, but moderately, or sips his wine with his meals," the lining membrane always becomes red and inflamed, and that "the blood-vessels of the inner surface are so far enlarged, as to be visible (to the naked eye), and distended with blood."

(*See Sewell's Plates, No. 2.*)

Dr. Sewell says that " in the stomach of the habitual drunkard, or hard drinker, the mucous or internal coat is in a state of irritation, with its blood-vessels, which are invisible while in a healthy state, enlarged and distended with blood, similar to the rum-blossoms sometimes seen on the face of the drunkard; and very frequently corroded with small ulcers, which are covered with white crusts, with the margins of the ulcers elevated and rugged."

(*See Sewell's Plates, No. 3.*)

He says that, " after a debauch of several

days, the internal or mucous surface of the stomach of the drunkard shows a high degree of inflammation, extending over the whole surface, changing its color to deep red, and in some points exhibiting a livid appearance."

(*See Sewell's Plates, No. 4.*)

He says that, with a great many "drunkards, or habitual hard drinkers, the stomach becomes thickened, and has large corroding cancers upon it."

(*See Sewell's Plates, No. 5.*)

He had a chance to dissect a large number of men who died of delirium tremens, and one or two of them prominent statesmen; and he says that he always found such stomachs "very much thickened and swollen, leaving but a small cavity for food, and this lined with a dark-brown flaky substance, which was really grumous blood, that had oozed out of the sores and cancers of the inflamed surface, and when this flaky substance was removed, the stomach looked quite dark, like an incipient state of mortification."

(*See Sewell's Plates, No. 6.*)

And again he says, "If the morbid effects of intemperance are in some degree various in different individuals; if they are not developed with the same degree of power and rapidity in one case as in another, — it is nevertheless true that alcohol is a poison forever at war with man's nature, and in all its forms and degrees of strength produces irritation of the stomach which is liable to result in inflammation, ulceration, and mortification, a thickening and induration of its coats, and, finally, scirrhus, cancer, and other organic affections; and it may be asserted with confidence, that no one who indulges habitually in the use of alcoholic drinks, whether in the form of wine or the more ardent spirits, possesses a healthy stomach."

Now, what do you think of the effects of alcohol upon the human stomach? Does it improve the condition of the stomach much?

Does it assist digestion very much? We fail to see it. If you say it does, you assume to know more than Dr. Sewell, who has spent his life in finding out.

The stomach is the great central office of the digestive system, and if that suffers, of course all the other organs must suffer! The whole man must suffer.

Let us hope that the people will learn these facts, and then act in accordance with what they have learned. Let us trust in the righteousness of our cause, the intelligence of the people, and our own powers of reason. Let us have faith in mankind, and confidence in public opinion; for these shall one day be the arbitrators of our cause.

LET US TRUST IN THE PEOPLE.

Now hundreds of thousands are falling around,
And the stars of our circle are under the ground,
Cut off in their vigor of manhood and prime,
And swept from the world and the borders of time;
Swept from the world by the Demon of Drink,
Deeply down in oblivious billows to sink.
Lost to themselves and their loved ones before,
Their final departure but few can deplore.

But millions on millions are waiting the dawn,
When all of these causes of woe shall be gone;
They are hopeful no longer to suffer delay,
But anxiously watching to welcome the day;
Anxiously watching and waiting for day,
When the sunshine of knowledge around them shall play,
When the drunkard's diseases and ills shall be o'er,
And men shall drink poison, to burn them, no more.

Will the time ever come? Will the day ever break?
Will the masses, misguided, their vices forsake?
And learn to be strong, to be hearty and hale,

Like the oak in the forest, unharmed by the gale?
Will the masses get knowledge, learn wisdom, and live?
The knowledge and wisdom that wiser men give?
Will they learn to give heed to the laws of their health?
The laws that bring vigor, and pleasure, and wealth?

Let us trust in the people. They're willing and strong
To banish a custom they've learned to be wrong.
Let us hope that the cause which we know to be right
They will gladly endorse, if we give them the light;
Let us wait for the time when the people shall rise,
And claim — and claim justly — the laws that are wise;
But while we are hoping, and waiting the hour,
Let us labor to teach them; — for knowledge is power!

IV.

ALCOHOL — WHAT EFFECT HAS IT UPON THE HUMAN BODY? — DOES IT EVER CAUSE DISEASE AND DEATH? — WHAT PART OF THE SYSTEM DOES IT INJURE? — HOW AND WHY?

(CONCLUDED.)

IV.

THIS is perhaps as good a time and place, as we shall find in which to explain the secret of the drunkard's insatiable appetite, — his gnawing, craving, burning desire for more liquor. Why this ungovernable thirst for more?

The reasons are plain. Did any of you ever have inflamed sore eyes? And do you remember how they itched and tingled and how you wanted to claw right into them with all your finger-nails and scratch them? How you wanted to irritate them? When you had rubbed and scratched and irritated them, they would, for a moment, feel easier — feel quiet and more comfortable. But do you not know that that same scratching, and gouging, and irritating, only inflamed them more, and made them worse afterwards, and harder to cure?

Now, the stomach, when once inflamed and sore from any cause, itches and tingles and burns in the same way, and feels uneasy, and wants to be scratched and rubbed and irritated. And when more alcohol is taken, which rubs and irritates the sore, it feels, for the time, more easy and quiet and satisfied. But the liquor thus taken to satiate this morbid burning for more, only irritates the sore, and inflames the stomach, and makes it worse and harder to heal, and more difficult to cure. Very few — old topers even — drink liquor because they love it. They drink it because it seems to allay this morbid itching and burning in the stomach. Anything that would irritate and scratch the inside of the stomach would allay that raging thirst the same as alcohol. Any other irritant poison would answer the purpose, and frequently does answer, as we shall show in another lecture on adulterations.

To cure this craving appetite, the victim should stop drinking at once, and totally abstain from all kinds of irritants, and restrict himself to a diet that will soothe and heal the soreness within. When the soreness gets entirely well, the appetite will entirely cease; and not before. Food that is easily digested will irritate the stomach but little, and therefore such food is always the best for the inebriate.

Once more to the task. Once more let us trace the havoc and ruin that alcohol brings upon the various organs of the body. After the stomach, what next?

The bowels, being a continuation of the digestive system, become inflamed and thickened, and sore and ulcerated, the same as the stomach. All the remarks heretofore made about the stomach apply also to the bowels, throughout their entire length. Thirty feet of sore, inflamed, ulcerated, and maturating bowels. What folly to burn one's insides in such a way, for the phantom pleasures of the wine-cup!

The liver becomes diseased also, and injured more than the stomach, — worse than the bowels.

Its effect upon the stomach and bowels, as we have seen, are terrible indeed; but Drs. Lallemand and Perrin, after a multitude of examinations, find the liver to be the most affected of all the organs, and the brain next. Letting the amount of alcohol found in the blood of the drunkard be represented by the figure one, they found in the substance of the brain one and one-third, and in the liver one and one-half. They found that the habitual drinker never has a healthy liver, but always inflamed and ulcerated, or else hardened and sore.

Listen to Dr. Sewell. "Alcohol produces a strong and speedy effect upon the liver. Its secretion often becomes changed from a bright yellow to a green or black, and from a thin fluid to a substance resembling tar in its consistence; and this change not unfrequently leads to the formation of biliary calculi, or gall stones. There often follows an enlargement of the organ, and a change in its structure, and in most cases studded with tubercles and ulceration. I have met with cases in which the liver has become so enlarged from intemperance, as to weigh from eight to twelve pounds, instead of four or five. I have also met with several cases, in which the liver had become shrivelled and indurated; its bloodvessels diminished, and the organ greatly changed in structure, the evident consequence of long-continued habits of intemperance."

Dr. Sewell has dissected so many of these besotted vagabonds, who swarm around the sink-holes of drunkenness at Washington City, that his word on that subject is almost the same as law.

What does he say about the kidneys? He says, "In the inebriate, these organs and the other organs immediately associated with them are seldom found in a healthy state." And why? Because the alcohol must go through the kidneys before it can get into the urine to pass off; and it inflames and burns and diseases them as it goes through.

And what does he say of the heart,— the most vital of all the organs of the body?

I give you his words: "From the fact that the heart sympathizes strongly with the stomach, and is so easily agitated by the passions which alcohol excites, and from several cases that I have dissected, I am inclined to think it seldom escapes uninjured in the habitual drunkard." And he gives a number of cases in proof, two of which I will give you: "A large athletic man — an old toper — drank a glass of raw whiskey, and fell instantly dead." On dissection it was found that the heart was spasmodically contracted, and the blood all squeezed out of it.

The other case was of a drunken public man, who, "while making a public speech, with his passions somewhat excited, fell instantly dead." When opened his heart was found cramped and pinched down to the smallest compass, and the blood all pinched out of it. The blood itself was loaded with alcohol, and the heart was making a herculean effort to throw it out, when the man perished.

And is this all? Not yet.' Not yet. Dr. Sewell says the lungs are diseased in two ways by ardent spirits. First, by inflaming the whole breathing apparatus, in being thrown off with the breath, "which often terminates in fatal bronchitis and consumption;" and "secondly, by the sympathy which is called into action between the lungs and other organs, — already in a state of disease, — and more especially the stomach and liver."

Well, is that all? Alas! not yet. The task before me is a dark, and deep, and sad one. But it shall be finished. The brain itself is diseased by alcohol. The heart, in trying to get rid of alcohol, throws too much blood (with alcohol mixed in it) into the brain; and this "inflames and engorges that organ. If this inflammation and engorgement is acute, it is usually attended with furious delirium." Do you hear that? Furious delirium! And now you know where the delirium tremens comes from, — inflammation and engorgement of the brain, by too much alcoholic blood.

Dr. Sewell says so. And Dr. Armstrong, an eminent physician of England, who possessed ample opportunities to find out, says so in these words: "I have found the free use of intoxicating liquors a frequent cause of chronic inflammation and engorgement of the brain, and its membranes.

Dr. Munroe says, "cases are on record of persons who, drinking off at a draft, from a quarter of a pint to a quart of ardent spirit, have died immediately afterwards. The poison having absorbed from the stomach, mixed with the blood, carried to the heart, and propelled to the brain, the nervous centres became at once paralyzed, and the heart ceased to beat."

Now, as the brain is the organ of the

mind, it follows that when that organ becomes inflamed, engorged, and diseased, that the mind must be disturbed and injured also, in many ways. The effect of alcohol upon the mind will be the subject of my next lecture.

Well, is this all? Not yet, my friends, not yet. Alcohol is a frequent cause of paralysis. Sometimes one leg is paralyzed, sometimes both, and sometimes one side of the body, and sometimes the other. This comes, very frequently, from alcoholic injury to the nerves, as seen in the tottering step and the trembling hand. The nerves are offshoots of the brain, and alcohol injures them in the same way that it does the brain; and it is from this cause that the drunkard reels and staggers and sees double.

Once more to the sickening, heart-revolting task. And here let me mention a disease called fatty degeneracy. Whenever muscle — hard, solid muscle — turns to fat, we call it fatty degeneracy. It is a very common disease among liquor-drinkers. They often look healthy in the face, and their limbs seem round and full; but the plumpness is no sign of strength. What should be muscle is turning into fat, and of course the person has less muscular power and strength. The muscle of the arms and legs partly turned to fat, and of course become soft, flabby, and weak. It is no longer muscle, but only fat. The blood gets loaded with fat, and the walls of the heart itself become fat, and it will by and by cease beating, — get sluggish, get tired, get softened, get sore, get filled with corruption, and stop.

Dr. Chambers says, " Alcohol produces fatty degeneracy more than any other agent. It impoverishes the blood; and there is no surer road to that fatty degeneration of muscular fibre, so much to be feared; and it is especially hurtful by bringing on disease of the heart."

Dr. F. R. Lees, of Leeds, England, in speaking of this, says, "That alcohol should produce, in drinkers, fatty degeneration of the blood, follows as a matter of course." There is a little fat in healthy blood, about from two to four parts in one thousand parts. But the eminent French analytical chemist, Lecann, found one hundred and seventeen parts in one thousand in drunkards' blood, — forty times as much as belonged there.

"Three-quarters of the chronic diseases of England," says Dr. Chambers, "and a large proportion in America, are in some way combined with fatty degeneracy, and chiefly with those who use ardent spirits."

And herein we have the reason why so

many liquor-drinkers look so plump and round in form. Their look of health is fictitious, for they die sooner, and more suddenly than spare men who drink no liquor. On this point I shall dwell at another time.

Now, let us hear Dr. Sewell's conclusion. His words are direct, and to the point; and no truer words have ever been penned: —

".But time would fail me, were I to attempt an account of half the pathology of drunkenness. Dyspepsia, jaundice, emaciation, corpulence, dropsy, ulcers, rheumatism, gout, tremors, palpitation, hysteria, epilepsy, palsy, lethargy, apoplexy, melancholy, madness, delirium tremens, and premature old age, compose but a small part of the catalogue of diseases produced by alcoholic drinks. Indeed, there is scarcely a morbid affection to which the human body is liable, that has not, in one way or another, been produced by them; there is not a disease but they have aggravated, nor a predisposition to disease which they have not called into action; and although their effects are in some degree modified by age and temperament, by habit and occupation, by climate and season of the year, and even by the intoxicating agent itself; yet the general and ultimate consequences are the same.

"The inebriate having, by the habitual use of alcoholic drinks, exhausted to greater or less extent the principle of excitability in the solids, the power of reaction, and the blood having become incapable of performing its offices also, he is alike predisposed to every disease, and rendered liable to the inroads of every invading foe. So far, therefore, from protecting the system against disease, intemperance ever constitutes one of its strongest predisposing causes.

"Superadded to this, whenever disease does lay its grasp upon the drunkard, the powers of life being already enfeebled by the stimulus of alcohol, he unexpectedly sinks in the contest, but too frequently to the mortification of his physician, and the surprise and grief of his friends. Indeed, inebriation so enfeebles the power of life, so modifies the character of disease, and so changes the operation of medical agents, that unless the young physician has studied thoroughly the constitution of the drunkard, he has but partially learned his profession, and is not fit for a practitioner of the present age.

"These are the reasons why the drunkard dies so easily, and from such slight causes.

"A sudden cold, a pleurisy, a fever, a fractured limb, or a slight wound of the skin, is often more than his shattered powers can endure. Even a little excess of exertion, an exposure to heat or cold, a hearty repast, or slight emotion of the mind, not unfrequently extinguishes the small remains of the vital principle.

"From a careful observation of this subject during many years of practice, I am persuaded that tens of thousands of temperate drinkers die annually of diseases through which the abstemious would pass in safety."

Thus you have the conclusions of the aged, venerable, experienced, and impartial Dr. Sewell.

"Well, but," says one, "Dr. Story, has anybody else come to these conclusions besides yourself, and Dr. Munroe, and Dr. Chambers, and Dr. Masing, and Dr. Lallemand, and Dr. Perrin, and Dr. Duroy, and Dr. Magendie, and Dr. McNish, and Dr.

Figg, and Dr. Thompson, and Dr. Tod, and Dr. Bowman, and Dr. Wood, and Dr. Beaumont, and Dr. Sewell, and Dr. Armstrong, and Dr. Lees, and Dr. Lecanu, — besides all these seventeen physicians, are there any others that agree with you as to the physiological effects of strong drink?"

I am happy to inform you, sir, that several others have come to the same conclusion.

Forty years ago, Dr. George B. Wood, in the United States Dispensatory, published these remarkable words, — and they are in the book, staring the people in the face, and have been ever since, in all the revised editions. Hear them: "As an article of daily use, alcoholic liquors produce the most deplorable consequences. Besides the moral degradation which they cause, their habitual use gives rise to dyspepsia, hypochondriasis, visceral obstructions, dropsy, paralysis, and not unfrequently mania."

These are his words. And there those words have stood, read by every druggist, and every doctor in the land (who reads at all) for forty years and more.

Will this nation ever listen to its wisest men? Or will it always follow the advice of third-rate upstarts, whose counsels lead to disease, disaster, and ruin?

Dr. John King, in his American Dispensatory, thus speaks, — and I would have you mark his words, for they are words of truth and candor: "In large quantities and continued daily, these (alcoholic) liquors occasion intoxication, nervous derangement, loss of appetite, mental imbecility, dyspepsia, indurated liver, granular disease of the kidneys, paralysis, mania, apoplexy, and death."

Hear that. What a catalogue of diseases!

Do you not believe these Dispensatories? You are bound to believe them because you have no other standard authorities. They are not disputed anywhere, by any responsible party.

The regular physicians all acknowledge the United States Dispensatory as authority; and the eclectics, and homœopaths, and Thompsonians, acknowledge the American Dispensatory as authority. And they have no other.

And the hydropaths surely all believe that alcohol is the source of a great many bodily diseases. Therefore, all the doctors of all the schools are bound to believe them true.

Dr. John C. Warren,. of Boston, has publicly endorsed all that Dr. Sewell has said about alcoholic diseases. He has done it in a public letter, which is published to the world.

Dr. Valentine Mott, of New York, has done the same thing, in the same way.

Dr. W. E. Horner, of Philadelphia,. has done the same.

Dr. Austin Flint, of Bellevue Hospital Medical College, city of New York, who is the author of a most able work, on the "Principles and Practice of Medicine," says, "In cases of chronic alcoholism, the digestive powers are weakened, the appetite is impaired, the muscular system is enfeebled, the generative functions decay, the blood is impoverished, and nutrition is imperfect and disordered, as shown by the flabbiness of the skin and muscle, and emaciation, or the abnormal accumulation of fat.

"The effects of alcohol enter directly into the causation of many affections, such as cirrosis of the liver, fatty liver, epilepsy (fits), muscular tremor, gastritis, pyrosis, various dyspeptic disorders, and various lesions of the kidney.

"Incidentally, alcohol favors the production of nearly all diseases, by lessening the power of resisting their causes, and contributes to their fatality by impairing the ability to tolerate and overcome them."

That is all sound doctrine, and right to the point. Dr. Flint, when he wrote that, was not writing a "temperance tract" for a "party of fanatics;" but a text-book, for the medical profession; and the profession has adopted the book.

And all the doctors know that these four gentlemen, Dr. Warren, Dr. Mott, Dr. Horner, and Dr. Flint, are first class authority, and their united opinion has almost the force of the law.

Dr. Broussais, a French physician, has made the same discoveries that Dr. Sewell did, by cutting open dead drunkards, and finding out for himself.

When George F. Cook, the drunken theatrical actor, died in New York, Dr. Hosack, of that city, dissected him, and found the liver frightfully diseased by alcohol.

Dr. Carpenter, the author of Carpenter's Physiology, has long since come to the same conclusions with Dr. Sewell and Dr. Broussais, and proclaimed them to the world.

Dr. Figg, of Edinburgh, Scotland, after a great number of examinations, has come to the same conclusions.

Dr. Munroe, of Hull, England, has come to the same conclusions, and gone, if possible, further still, in condemning the use of alcoholic liquors.

Dr. Baker has examined and experimented extensively, and arrived at the same conclusions.

Dr. Virchow has also been examining the blood of drunkards, and finds it loaded with fat, and disease, and in a state of premature decay, from the use of alcohol.

Dr. Ogle has made one hundred and forty-three post mortem examinations of drunkards, and found over a hundred of their hearts softened by fatty degeneracy; and the other organs in a state of disease, the same as described by Dr. Sewell,— all from the use of alcohol.

Dr. Markham, editor of the British Medical Journal, — which is authority everywhere,— has had both sides of the question published in his Journal lately, holding himself neutral. But he has come out with his casting vote, giving what he calls " the grand practical conclusions." And what are they?

" 1st. That alcohol is not food; and that,

being simply a stimulant (irritant), its use is hurtful to the body of a healthy man.

"2. That if the use of it be of service, it is so only to a man in an abnormal condition; and that our duty, as men of medicine, is to find out what those abnormal conditions are."

He seems to doubt whether it ought to be used even as a medicine.

And that from the London Medical Journal, in the editorial column, — is not that strong authority? Do you want more?

I have oceans of it, and the very best; but shall only refer now to a little more.

Professor Lehman, the great chemist, and author of a book on chemistry, is out against alcohol in any form. He says he "does not believe it is capable of contributing anything toward maintaining life." That knocks it, both as a food and a medicine.

Dr. John Higginbottom, of the Royal College of Surgeons, England, after sixty years of practice, has published a work, from which I quote. "Alcohol has no specific effect on any organ of the body, for the cure of any disease. On the contrary, the taking of it is a principal cause of disease. Every disease is aggravated by it, and many are generated by the use of it. I consider it impious in any medical man saying that any constitution requires alcoholic stimulants."

Dr. Brinton, physician in Saint Thomas's Hospital, is out against alcohol, in all its forms, as positively as any heretofore named.

Dr. Gardner, Professor of Practice in the University of Glasgow, Scotland, and Surgeon to the Royal Infirmary, has had six hundred cases of typhus fever under his care. One-half he treated in the usual way, with tinctures or medicines, with alcohol in them, and lost seventeen out of a hundred. The other half he treated with the same medicines, leaving the alcohol out, and only lost twelve in a hundred: showing that the difference between seventeen and twelve, which is five out of every hundred of the sick people, have been murdered with alcoholic medicine.

Dr. James B. Kirk, Teacher of Surgery, and Professor of Chemistry, in the Greenock Institution of Arts and Sciences, speaking of alcoholic diseases, comprehended in drunkenness, says they are "by far more destructive than any plague which ever raged in Christendom, — more malignant than any other epidemic pestilence which ever devastated our suffering race, whether in the shape of the burning and contagious typhus, the loathsome and mortal small-pox, the cholera of the East, or the yellow fever of the West; a disease by far more loathsome, infectious, and destructive than all of them put together with all their dread array of sufferings and of death united in one ghastly assemblage of horrific and appalling misery." And again, speaking of bilious complaints he says that a very large share of them are " only the effect of an irritated and diseased liver resulting from the repetition of alcoholic stimulus; and then comes wasting of the strength, and emaciation of the body, premature old age, uselessness and helplessness, till dropsy kindly releases the wretch from that vulture which ever preys upon him, and devours the more greedily as it reaches the vitals of its victims."

And the able and talented Dr. Wm. Sweetster, of Vermont, tells us that " we gain nothing, then, by the employment of ardent spirits; but how much do we not lose? I could trace, in forbidding relief, the shattered nerves, the tottering limbs, the gnawing of the vulture at the liver, gout with its maddening pain, bloated dropsy, the wild ravings of insanity, wasting consumption, apoplexies and palsies oppressing the brain, and rendering the limbs powerless."

The declarations of Dr. Kirk and Dr. Sweetster come down to us through thirty years of time, and all these years have proved their declarations true.

As to whether it is good for medicine, I am going, once more, to quote from the United States Dispensatory: —

"In some states of acute disease," — mark that. How cautious Dr. Wood is! — "in some states of acute disease, characterized by excessive debility, alcohol is a valuable remedy. But in chronic diseases, physicians should be cautious in prescribing liquors containing it."

He does not recommend it very highly; but tells physicians to be cautious in using it. On this point let me quote, also, from the American Dispensatory: "There are very few cases in which alcoholic stimulants are given, and these are never of a chronic character."

Dr. King is positive. "Never of a chronic character."

These views and conclusions are thoroughly and heartily endorsed by Dr. Massey, the chemist, Dr. Duroy, the chemist, Dr. Lallemand of France, and Dr. Perrin of France; and these are backed by Dr. James McCulloch, of Scotland, and Dr. Edward Smith, of London, all of whom endorse all that we have said concerning alcoholic diseases, and all of whom unite in saying that "alcohol should be prescribed medicinally as carefully as any other poisonous agent."

Thus we have the additional testimony of Dr. King, and Dr. Warren, and Dr. Mott, and Dr. Horner, and Dr. Flint, and Dr. Broussais, and Dr. Hosack, and Dr. Carpenter, and Dr. Baker, and Dr. Virchow, and Dr. Ogle, and Dr. Higginbottom, and Dr. Kirk, and Dr. Sweetster, and Dr. Markham, and Dr. Lehman, and Dr. Brinton, and Dr. Gardner, and Dr. McCulloch, and Dr. Smith, — twenty first-class physicians, in addition to the seventeen heretofore mentioned, — in all thirty-seven strong minds from the medical and chemical profession. Their united opinion is a tremendous force, — an irresistible power, — moving like the in-coming tide of the sea, lifting mighty navies, as if they were but toys, and advancing beyond and above the low-water mark of the olden time.

From them we learn these tremendous lessons: That the effect of alcohol upon the human body is that of an irritant and a poison. That it burns, and inflames, and ulcerates, and injures every organ that it touches. That the stomach, and bowels, and blood, and heart, and lungs, and liver, and kidneys, and muscle, and brain are all injured and diseased. That no part of the drunkard's body is free from disease, but all parts inflamed and cancerous and corrupt with sores. That the anger and ferocity of the diseases and ulcers is in proportion to the quantity of alcohol consumed. That it does not contain any of the elements of food, and therefore is not useful in developing bone, nor muscle, nor blood, nor brain, nor any part of the human body, but is an absolute injury to all parts. That it dissolves the juices of the body, and hinders and prevents digestion. That even as a medicine, it should never be used in chronic cases, under any circumstances. That it is used as a medicine only in acute cases; and then only when they are characterized by great prostration. And that it should be prescribed with as much care and caution as any other poisonous agent.

And besides all these injuries and diseases, — the catalogue and description of which sickens and palls the stoutest heart, — besides all these, you all know how the drunkard is exposed to the filthy air of basement saloons, exposed to the rain and the snow, and the midnight storms, which aggravate his injuries; how he misses his regular food and loses his regular sleep, when he is drunk, all of which are contrary to the laws of bodily health; and how his sleep is disturbed, — when he does sleep, — with frightful dreams and horrid visions, and wakes without being rested or refreshed, which is very injurious to his physical health, and hastens the day of his death, and adds pains and anguish to the sorrows of his dying hour.

Do you want more testimony still? You shall have it, for I want you to be convinced. This time the proof shall come from the medical profession, combined in force, and a strong array.

The Medical Society of the State of New York — the physicians of a whole great State — have spoken, by passing, unanimously, this resolution: "Resolved, that, in view of the ravages made upon the morals, health, and property of the people of this State, by the use of alcoholic drinks, it is the opinion of this medical society, that the moral, sanitary, and pecuniary condition of the State, would be promoted by the passage of a Prohibitory Law."

There it is, in plain letters, and positive words. And shall the doctors of a whole State pronounce their opinion in vain?

I wish you to notice where the great and impartial brain of the medical profession to be found, and whether it is drifting.

I present one more set of resolutions. Let the lovers of temperance and good order hear and take courage. The world is moving, and moving in the right direction.

The following opinion has been signed by Dr. Carpenter, author of Carpenter's Physiology, and five thousand more, first-class physicians:—

"We, the undersigned, are of opinion,

"1. That a very large proportion of human misery, including poverty, disease and crime, is induced by the use of alcoholic or fermented liquors as beverages.

"2. That the most perfect health is compatible with total abstinence from all such intoxicating beverages, whether in the form of ardent spirits, or as wine, beer, ale, porter, cider, etc.

"3. That persons accustomed to such drinks may, with perfect safety, discontinue them entirely, either at once, or gradually after a short time.

"4. That total and universal abstinence from alcoholic beverages of all sorts would add greatly to the health, the prosperity, the morality, and the happiness of the human race."

Do you want stronger language or more emphatic? Who has a better right to know than the doctors have? Attached to that opinion, are the names of five thousand doctors, chemists, and druggists. And is the united voice of five thousand professional men to be disregarded? How long? Oh, how long?

Great bodies move slowly, and the men who are engaged in learning, practising, and teaching the laws of life and health, have been slow in expressing their opinion.

But now, since they have pronounced their opinion, it should ring in tones of thunder all over the land.

WE HAVE JOINED YOUR NOBLE ARMY.

We have searched the realms of nature — far and wide our
    search has spread;
We have analyzed the products that compose our daily bread;
And examined all the organs of the living and the dead,
But we fail to find an organ in the human body laid,
Or an appetite in nature, in its native form arrayed,
That requires, for its promotion, any alcoholic aid!

We have studied all diseases, as the faithful only can,
That have blighted human pleasure, since the dawn of time
    began;
In all their many windings, through the fragile frame of man,
But we fail to find an evil, or a pain, in all the field,

Or disease, mild or malignant, whether open or concealed,
That requires the poison alcohol, to hasten it to yield.

We have found, in all our studies, that the poison is a blight,
That enfeebles every organ, burns its vigor, rots its might,
And that darkens all the future, with the heavy pall of night;
That it certainly exposes (thus the book of nature saith)
Its victims to diseases, that will steal away their breath,
And drag them down, in sorrow, to the iron gates of death!

You have waited for our counsels; waited patiently and long;
For the voice of careful science to denounce the giant wrong;
And it has our condemnation, earnest, ponderous, and strong!
We have joined your noble army, with the strength that in us
   lies,
To subdue the fell destroyer, that the laws of health defies,
And to urge the war, with vigor, till the giant evil dies!

V.

Alcohol — What Effect has it upon the Immortal Mind? — Does it ever cause Indolence, Ignorance, or Depravity? — Is it ever the Cause of Mania, Insanity, Madness, Lunacy, Delirium, Wickedness, or Crime? — Does it increase the Number of Dolts, Idiots, and Fools? — In what Way? — and Why?

V.

WE are now about to enter a field that has never yet been fully explored; about to investigate the brain, with its wonderful and beautiful mechanism, and ascertain the effect of alcohol upon the immortal soul.

Let us proceed thoughtfully and cautiously.

It is now admitted by everybody that the brain is the organ of the mind. It is not the mind itself, but only the organ through which the mind acts, and without which there would be no mind, without which no man could think or feel. Just as the muscle is the organ of strength. The muscle is not strength, but only the organ through which strength is manifested, and without which there would be no strength.

The lung is not heat, but only the organ by means of which heat is generated for the body, and without which the body could have no warmth.

The stomach is not food, but only the kitchen where the food is prepared for the nourishment of the whole system, and without which food would be of no service.

The blood is not the life of man, but only the organ that takes the food, when prepared by the stomach, carries supplies to every part of the system, and furnishes to each department the means by which life is sustained, and without which there could be no life.

In like manner the brain is the organ of the mind, or the medium through which the mind is made manifest. And hence a brief description of the brain, will throw immense light upon the subject before us. That the brain is the organ of the mind has been abundantly proved by Dr. Gall, and Dr. Spurzheim, and Dr. Combe, Professor Fowler, and others; and there are at this time, few if any, who doubt the fact. Dr. Gray, in his great work on anatomy, says: "The size of the brain appears to bear a general relation to the intellectual capacity of the individual. An idiot's brain weighs only a pound and a quarter, or a pound and a half; while the brain of a highly intellectual man, at maturity, weighs three and a half or four pounds, or more.

"The brains of animals are very small, when compared with the brains of man.

"The brain of a large whale that is seventy-five feet long, weighs only about five pounds. The brain of the largest elephant weighs only about eight pounds. And these are the only two animals in God's creation that have a brain in equal weight to that of a man." And I may add to the statements of Dr. Gray, that the brain of the whale and the elephant, as well as all other animals, is of a much coarser material, and more loosely put together than the fine-spun, and closely woven brain of man.

The brain of some people is finer, and made of better material than that of other people, just as oak is better material than buckeye, and mahogany is finer than oak. But the human brain is almost always superior to the brain of an animal.

Dr. Romberg, of Germany, says, " The brain is the organ of the soul."

Most animals' brains weigh less than the human idiot, besides being of a very inferior material.

The human brain, when viewed as a mass, is of a grayish white, or chalk color, and it is very similar to the marrow that you have seen in the marrow bones of animals. It is made up of very minute white threads or strands called nerves, which are very small and very delicate in their nature, — many of them finer then the finest hair, — as fine as the spider's web and finer, many of them being so fine that they cannot be seen without the aid of a magnifying-glass. They run from the head to every part of the body, or rather from every part of the body to the head.

One little nerve starts from the end of your fingers, and runs the whole length of your arm, and passing through the neck reaches the head. Another, starting from the tip of your toe, runs the whole length of the leg, passes into the hollow of the backbone, reaches all the way up the spinal column, and finally winds its way through the neck and into the head. Another starts from the stomach, and, winding its way through the chest and neck, enters the head also. Every part of the body is supplied with little fine nerves, and they all take the shortest and easiest route to the head.

We may catch the idea, perhaps, by comparing the whole system of nerves to a system of telegraphs, coming into a great city. One little wire starts from Portland, Maine, and is mounted on a myriad of poles passing over hills and across villages, through forests and over prairies, till it reaches Chicago. Another starts from New Orleans, and winds along the Mississippi Valley, half the length of a continent, till it reaches Chicago. And another little bit of a wire starts from San Francisco, stretches across the desert, climbs the mountains, reaches beyond the plains, till it comes to Chicago also. Along these little wires comes the news from every quarter of the country. So with these little fine nerves. They start from every corner of the body, and all come to the head — as the great central office. They are the organs of sensation and feeling, and they bring the news from every part of the body to the head. Touch the end of your finger to a hot stove, and instantly the news is sent along the nerve to the head, that the finger is being burned, and the head sends back a despatch to remove the finger. Set your bare foot upon a thorn, and a despatch is sent to the head and back in the same way. Take a bite of Indian turnip in your mouth, and a despatch is instantly sent to the head, along the nerve leading from the mouth to the head, and peremptory orders are sent promptly back to spit it out. If you could take a knife and reach into your arm at the elbow, and cut off all the nerves that pass that point, you could then hold your hand in the fire, and let it broil and fry, and it would give you no pain; nor could you open nor shut your fingers, nor take your hand out of the fire, without using some other part of your body. Reach in at the knee, and cut off all the nerves that pass that point, and then you could put your foot into boiling water, and cook it until the flesh should fall off the bones, and you would not feel it; nor could you take it out of the water, nor move a toe, unless you take your hand to lift it out. Cut off all the nerves that start from your mouth, and you could fill your mouth with nitric acid, and hold it there, and it would not pain you; nor could you spit it out, unless you should lean over your head and just let it run out itself. So you see that the nerves are the organs of feeling and motion, and without them we could neither feel nor move.

As these little nerves start from every conceivable part of the body, they must be very numerous. You can scarcely touch yourself anywhere, with a needle, without touching upon a nerve. You may count the hairs of your head, perhaps, but you never can count the nerves, so great is their number. When you look at a piece of fresh meat, you do not see many of the nerves, because they are too small to be seen.

As these little nerves approach toward the head, they run together side by side, forming larger strands or threads, so that you can more easily see them with the naked eye.

The nerves of the thumb and little finger, and all the fingers, get together part way up the arm, so as to form a chord as large as a small needle. And others, coming from the stomach and bowels, join with those near the neck, forming a chord larger than the largest knitting-needle. So the nerves coming from the feet run together and form chords or ropes, and these again unite with others, forming larger ropes, until they all approach the neck, where they are found in twenty-four large ropes or cables. And these again unite, two running together into one, so as to form twelve very large cables,. called the Twelve Pairs of Nerves.

And here let us notice a wonderful and beautiful peculiarity of all the nerves. They are nearly or quite twice as long as the body they traverse. For instance, you are six feet high, the nerves that run from your feet will be twice six, which is twelve feet long. If from the end of your finger to your head is four feet, the nerve will be about twice four, which is eight feet long, and so on.

If there were a hole in the top of your head, so that the nerves could be carried upward, some of them would reach six feet above your head. And then suppose some person could commence at the top of them, and coil them up into nice little coils, and wrap them in pretty little bundles, and reel some of them in the sweetest little skeins, like skeins of silk, only finer, and wind some of them into little spiral coils, like the thread on a spool, only so much nicer and finer, and turn some of them into nice, tiny loops; and then take all these little coils and bundles, and skeins and loops, and pass them down gently, through the supposed hole in your head, and pack them away side by side, and on the top of each other, until the skull should be packed solid and full of little coils and bundles, and skeins and loops. Wouldn't it be nice to see them all packed away so sweetly? Well, if you ever get a chance to see the doctor dissect a human brain, that is just what you will see.

You will see that the human brain is only

the upper half of all the nerves, wrapped into the most exquisite little packages, and bunches, and laid away in the skull, in the most bewitching little layers. Some places you will see little thin partitions skilfully placed in between the little layers and packages, — thin as the thinnest paper, and thinner, and in other places they will be lying snugly together, and just gently touching each other, without anything between them. Wonderful and beautiful is the structure of the human brain!

But you ought to have a magnifying glass when you look at the human brain, because to the naked eye, it looks about like the marrow in a marrow-bone. And it is the same thing as marrow. Because the marrow in the bone is only a straw, or a number of straws of nerves, running toward the head. That part of the nerve which is coiled up in the skull, we call brain; and that part of the brain which is outside of the head, reaching all over the body like little telegraphs, we call nerves. So that the nerves and the brain are essentially the same thing.

You remember what Mrs. Partington told Ike, when he was lying down on the lounge, with his feet on the table. She told him that he ought not to lie that way, because his brains might happen to all run down into his head.

I think I have seen a few persons who, to all appearances, had by far the larger half of their brains located in their bodies.

The phrenologists made a great mistake when they undertook to make the science of the mind independent of physiology; because the mind is only the manifestation of intelligence and goodness, or the opposite of these, made through the brain, one-half which is spread through all parts of the body. And the physiologists but very imperfectly understand the whole system of man, until they have mastered the mysterious and wonderful workings of the mind or soul, through and beyond the nerves and brain.

The science of the body and the science of the mind are together but one science, and should be called the science of human life.

The brain, like all other parts of the body, is supplied by the blood. It was for ages supposed that there were no blood-vessels in the body of the brain. But it is now well understood by all physicians that the brain is abundantly supplied with arteries and veins. They are so fine that few of them are visible. But when we take the magnifying glass and examine carefully, we find myriads of arteries and veins. They are finer than the finest hairs,

— finer than the web of the spider, — finer than the nerves themselves, and yet hollow and filled with blood. These little arteries entwine their little branches all around and all through the coils and skeins of nerves, in a thousand directions; so that the brain is fed by the blood directly from the heart. And as the heart gets the food directly from the stomach, it follows that the brain is supplied from the food that we eat and the fluids that we drink passing from the stomach into the heart, and propelled by that organ directly to the brain itself! It follows, therefore, that if the stomach and heart become diseased, and the blood diseased and loaded with impurities, that the brain is supplied — if supplied at all — with impure materials and diseased food.

The brain asks for bread, and for meat, and the blood brings it sour bread, and decayed meat, that have just come through a diseased and ulcerated stomach, a softened and sore heart, along a line of arteries, the inside lining of which is inflamed and mattering. Now, can a brain be healthy thus supplied with filthy food? How can a mind be sound that has to act through a starved and diseased brain?

We have shown, in a former lecture, how alcohol diseases the stomach, and diseases the heart, and how it thickens the blood with corruption and disease; therefore it must follow that the brain is supplied with thick and depraved blood. The little arteries of the brain are so small that the thick and diseased blood of the drunkard will not pass into them, without being forced in, by a too great exertion of the heart. This engorges the brain, and stretches the little arteries too full, distends them beyond their natural size, and strains them, and this causes pressure against the nearest nerves, and this pressure injures or destroys the ability to feel and move and think. When the man feels and moves and thinks imperfectly we say he is drunk. When he cannot think, nor feel, nor move at all, we say he is dead drunk.

Sometimes the alcohol burns and scorches these little blood-vessels through which it passes, until they become charred and shrivelled and crisped and harder and smaller than they should be; so that the thick, grumous, and diseased blood of the inebriate cannot pass through them at all, and even healthy blood will not enter them. Some thin fluid like alcohol, or chloroform, or ether may pass them perhaps, but blood cannot.

Sometimes the alcohol, in these dried-up and parched-up arteries and veins, oozes out through the cracks and crevices in them, into the substance of the brain itself, causing it to turn to fat or grease, and look like little drops of oil or lard, instead of strands of nerve or brain. This is called fatty degeneracy of the brain, and is quite common among liquor-drinkers.

Sometimes these arteries burst, and the blood mixes right in among the brain, forming clots, which make sores in the body of the brain itself; and of course destroys a few of the neighboring nerves that are around the sores. And these clots of blood, from the bursted arteries, press so hard upon the surrounding brain, as to cause paralysis, palsy, and death, as we have heretofore shown, and injure these beautiful little arteries of the brain itself, making them sore in all their myriad little branches.

If the person stops drinking, the blood that has thus run out into the brain will generally be absorbed, the bursted vessel heal up, and the brain get well; but more frequently the blood thus run out will dry into a hard, solid clot, causing a permanent injury, or else the brain close to it will turn to pus or matter, and make a filthy, mattery sore right in the brain itself, that is difficult to heal.

Do you suppose that a substance that is so poisonous as to burn a stomach until it is fiery-red and purple and sore, — a substance that is not modified by digestion, but remains the same, a poison, as long as it remains in the system, — a substance that, being thinner than blood, will readily pass into the little arteries of the brain, propelled there by the heart while it is making herculean efforts to get rid of the poison itself, — do you suppose such a poison does not inflame and ulcerate the little tender arteries of the brain? Such a substance could not fail, and does not fail, to injure the brain seriously. Dissection shows the little arteries of the brain to be strained, irritated, inflamed, engorged, ulcerated, and often bursted by the poisonous effects of alcohol! The arch-destroyer leaves a fiery path on his journey through the brain! And the mind that has to act through such a brain must be injured in proportion!

When alcohol is taken into the stomach, its presence is telegraphed along the nerves to the brain. This is rather a pleasant sensation — and the only pleasant sensation worth mentioning — caused by the alcohol, which is so volatile and penetrating in its nature that a part of it penetrates through the coatings of the stomach, along the pathway of the nerves, and follows those nerves to the brain. But by far the largest portion of the alcohol takes the natural, open channels, out of the stomach, into the heart, through the arteries, directly to every part of the body and brain. This, of course, stimulates at first, or, to use more appropriate language, irritates and burns the brain into greater activity!

And now comes the question, What part of the brain does it stimulate or irritate the most? In answering this question let me compare the arteries of the head to the limbs and branches of a beautiful shade-tree. Just a little way above the ground the limbs and branches are quite large, but as they go upward they divide and subdivide, getting smaller and smaller and more numerous, until, toward the top of the tree, they get to be very small and slender twigs.

So with the arteries of the head. In the lower part of the head they are quite large, — so large that they can easily be seen with the naked eye, — but they divide and subdivide, getting smaller and smaller, and finer and finer, and more numerous, as they approach toward the top and front of the head, where they are extremely minute. It follows, therefore, that there will be the most alcohol where the arteries are the largest, and consequently all the lower part of the brain will be stimulated or irritated the most; and, as the brain is the organ of the mind or soul, the lower organs of the mind or soul will be stimulated to the greatest activity, and the higher organs of the intellect, mind, or soul, will be stimulated the least. Is not that perfectly rational?

Well, now what are some of the lower organs of the mind that become stimulated most? The desire to drink is one of the lower organs, and when it has been stimulated, the man wants to drink again,—wants to drink when by nature he would not be dry,—wants to drink what a normal nature does not require, and what does not quench thirst. The desire to drink becomes a mania, and he knows not when to stop!

The desire to attack is one of the lower organs, and when irritated by poison the man wants to attack, perhaps, his nearest and dearest friends; and, if the organ is already large in his organization, he wants to break, burn, destroy, and kill; will want to quarrel and fight with his neighbors; will want to break, burn, and destroy his neighbor's property; will want to beat and abuse the wife of his bosom, and punish and abuse the children of his loins! Wife-beating and child-beating have become so common among drinking people that they have ceased to become matters of surprise, but are expected and looked for as matters of course. Dr. Munroe mentions a case, where "a man, who was peaceable when sober, kicked down a loving and beseeching wife with as much vengeance as he would kick a reptile out of his way, and then thrashed his poor little helpless children, and tore the clothes from their little, innocent bodies to pawn for more drink!"

Is not this mania? What is mania? Webster, in his big dictionary, says mania is "Violent derangement of the mind, madness, insanity, excessive or unreasonable desire, insane passion." I infer, therefore, that if a person has an inclination to do an unnatural and wrong act, and that inclination is beyond the control of his will, such an inclination or desire thus irresistible and uncontrollable is mania.

A mechanic in New York city told me that when he was out of sight and reach of liquor, he did not very much desire it; but when he saw it, he wanted it greatly; that after he had taken the least taste of it, he could not control his desire for more; and that when he had partaken freely, and was at home, he felt an almost superhuman inclination to kill his wife! With tears in his eyes he said that he loved his wife as dearly as any man could, but several times while intoxicated he had caught himself with weapons in his hands preparing to take her life, and had to hasten from her presence to prevent himself from doing so! He said he did not want to be guilty of such an awful crime, and tried to banish the thought, but feared that some day he might commit the crime before he was aware of it! This case represents a double mania: mania to drink, followed by a mania to kill! And whenever the forms of mania multiply it becomes insanity or madness. Webster says that insanity is "Unsoundness of mind, derangement of intellect, synonymous with lunacy, madness, derangement, alienation, aberration, mania, delirium, frenzy, monomania, dementia." Well, that definition covers pretty extensive ground. And he defines madness to be "Disorder of intellect; infatuation, with excitement of perception, wildness of passion, fury, rage."

When John Girdwood was on the scaffold, and about to be hung, he said to the people: "Fellow-men, before God, in whose presence I shall stand in a few minutes, I would as soon have taken my own life, as that of my dear boy, for I loved my wife and children as dearly as any man could do; but I was maddened by the drink, and knew not what I was doing!"

When Dr. Pitchard, of Glasgow, was about to be executed for poisoning his wife and mother-in-law, he confessed that "being somewhat excited by whiskey, I yielded to the temptation to give them sufficient chloroform to cause death. I can assign no motive for the conduct which actuated me, beyond a species of terrible madness and the use of ardent spirits!"

After Wilkes Booth, had made up his mind to kill President Lincoln, he could not muster the courage to execute his plan, until after he went again into a restaurant and called for "brandy! brandy!" Only after the organ of attack was irritated by alcohol, dared he to murder one of the noblest, best, and greatest men of modern times.

Some, when they have poisoned their brain with alcohol, are haunted with a strong desire to commit suicide, and will watch for weeks and months for a chance to make way with themselves. The melancholy mania for suicide often accompanies the mania to kill.

Dr. Munroe tells us that he once knew a laboring man, who, " when he had taken a few glasses of ale, would chuckle with delight at the thought of firing a certain gentleman's stacks. When his brain was free from the poison, a more quiet or better disposed man could not be. He afterwards fired the stacks of his employer, and served fifteen years in prison for doing so. Many a person, otherwise well disposed, has fired a house, a barn, or a boat, or a bridge, through this same mania to burn, which often follows the mania to drink.

You have, perhaps, all witnessed exhibitions of the drunkard's mania to break. In the saloon he will break tumblers, decanters, and pitchers, or his fellow-topers' skull, and then come home and smash the lamps and looking-glasses, kick over the table and dishes, throw the chairs through the window, and kick down the clock, and play smash generally.

Pat came home one night drunk, and pushed over the cupboard and broke all the dishes, and spilt all the cold victuals, and his wife Bridget, who had also partaken of a "wee drop," took down the looking-glass and broke it over his head, saying, "Bloody wars, and it's mysilf that'll be afther breakin' furniture wid ye, time about!"

The organ of acquisition, or desire to get, possess, and accumulate, is also one of the lower organs of the brain, traversed by some of the larger arteries of the brain. And you all know how common it is for drinkers to be found with a mania to steal.

A wealthy merchant of Chicago tells me that he has a lady customer, who is in affluent circumstances, and abundantly able to pay for all her needs, but who frequently comes to his store when under the influence of liquor, to purchase goods, and rarely fails to conceal some article of value about her person before she leaves. A few days after, when the influence of the poison has ceased to operate, she sends the goods back. She has confessed to the merchant, that, after drinking ardent spirit, she cannot resist the inclination that comes in her way. Sending back the goods proves that she is honest when sober. Taking them proves that she is dishonest when muddled. The lower organ of acquisition is stimulated to excessive activity, while conscience or moral honesty and the will are both located at the top of the head, where the arteries are very small, and not stimulated in proportion. The police reports are loaded with cases of larceny and theft committed under the influence of liquor. Cases of this kind are so numerous, that it is hardly necessary to mention any of them. Out of the mania to steal and the mania to cheat comes the mania to gamble. Many who would scorn to stake money on a game of chance when sober, will be eager to gamble for money on a game of cards or billiards just as soon as they have inflamed the organ of acquisition and policy, which makes them want to get and acquire by strategy and cunning.

The irritation of the organs of acquisition and attack, coupled with the mania to steal and gamble, very easily develop the mania to rob. How often does the defeated gambler, with his brain inflamed with whiskey, rise from the gambling-table, with a mind bent on robbing the successful one before he reaches home! Deliberate, premeditated robberies are comparatively scarce; but robberies under the influence of liquor are by far too numerous.

Close in this connection comes the mania to lie. The side organ of sublimity, which makes a man love great things and want to do great things, and the front organ of language, which makes people want to talk, are both stimulated considerably, while honesty, at the top of the head, and judgment and reason, at the top and front of the head, are less stimulated. Hence the enormous, outrageous lies that tipsy men will tell. They will lie, and then chuckle and gloat over the enormity of their falsehoods; take a special delight in telling the most shallow and silly but monstrous lies.

Again: the organ of amativeness or sexual love is one of the lower organs, through which pass some of the larger arteries; and when these arteries are filled with poisoned and corrupted blood, the person will be possessed with a mania for lust. The brothel is close to the groggery. Young men go out of the house of tippling to the house of prostitution. Husbands who drink the poison draught, are apt to prove faithless to their marriage vows. Wives who drink to intoxication want only opportunity to commit adultery. No married person can long put faith in a drunken companion. Some persons quaff the poison liquid on purpose to produce this mania for lust; but they generally live long enough to regret the act with shame and remorse. The way of the transgressor is hard, and persons who drink to intoxication, for such an object, soon find there are bitter dregs in the cup of folly.

On account of the lower organs being so unduly excited, and the higher organs of reason, judgment, conscience, and will, not being equally excited so as to control them, the man ceases to be himself, is directed and impelled by his lower organs and passions, and becomes obedient only to the powers and forces of evil! Is not this depravity? What is depravity? Webster says that depravity is "the state of being depraved or corrupted; a vitiated state of mind or character; want of virtue, absence of religious feeling or principle, extreme wickedness." Such is the definition of depravity; and where can we find depravity more complete than among inebriates.

Time will not allow me to notice all the forms of mania that are developed by intoxication, for they are too numerous. Mania has many forms. Alcohol does not affect all people's minds, nor control their actions alike. And why? Because the shape and size of people's brains are not alike. As a general rule the organs of the brain that are large, healthy, and active, have larger arteries running through them, and are better supplied with blood from the heart, than the smaller organs. It follows, therefore, that the organs already large and active will generally be irritated for a time into greater activity. One man has large self-esteem, and when he gets drunk, the self-esteem becomes more active, and forthwith he thinks he is a nobleman or a king. He undertakes to prove it by acting grand and lordly, as he thinks, and is reckless with his money, to prove that he is rich.

The efforts of a drunken man to be grand and kingly are so ridiculous that they call to mind the efforts made by three journeymen tailors in London, who got together and issued a proclamation, commencing, " We the people of England, in mass convention assembled ! "

One has the organ of ambition large, and is fond of applause. When he gets drunk he undertakes eloquence. One of this kind addressed a hitching-post, a telegraph-pole, and a wooden Indian, in front of a cigar store, as follows : " Gentlemen, fellow (hic) citizens, this is an unexpected (hic) ovation ! It is not my own merit, but the cause I (hic) represent, which gives me this enthusiastic (hic) reception. I bid you an affectionate fare (hic) well."

Another prides himself on his muscular strength, and he essays to show it. Dr. Munroe saw a young man who had exhausted himself in performing what he called "great deeds of daring and valor." He had gathered two door-knockers, three bell-pulls, and a stairway railing, all of which he had pulled off by main strength, and collected during the night.

An intoxicated man, the other day in Chicago, imagined himself a locomotive; thought his head was cow-catcher, and his arms were driving-wheel pitmans. While going along the street, saw two policemen ahead. Whistled to them. Hallooed to them to get off the track. As they failed to get off, he run into them with his cow-catcher, and knocked them down with his pitmans. Next day the judge fined him five dollars for running his locomotive on the pavement.

A crowd of guzzlers get together to guzzle. One feels musical, and undertakes to sing. To him the music is magnificent; and to his tipsy companions, delightful. But to a sober, sensible man, the music is flat, insipid, discordant, harsh, and stale.

Others among them say things they supposed to be witty, and they all laugh heartily at each other's brilliancy. But if they could hear the same stuff read, after the poison in their brains had ceased to operate, they would not call it wit nor brilliancy. Too soft, too coarse, too flat, too vulgar for either. It would hardly pass for tenth-rate bosh.

Alcohol dulls the edge, and takes away the keenness and clearness of the mind. The eye is not so quick to perceive, nor the ear so keen to hear, nor the reason so accurate or quick to comprehend, nor the judgment so quick to decide, nor the will so ready to command, nor the memory so tenacious to retain.

Health without stimulation affords the greatest amount of mental and physical power. Dr. Brinton says, "Mental acuteness, accuracy of perception, and delicacy of the senses are all so far opposed to the action of alcohol, that the greatest efforts of each are incompatible with the drinking of any moderate quantity of fermented liquid."

And if the mind becomes inaccurate, unbalanced, sluggish, and beclouded, is it not depraved? Depravity, remember, is "The state of being depraved, corrupted, or vitiated, in mind or character."

And we remark, many of these forms of mania and depravity, which are at first but temporary, lasting only during the drunken debauch, finally become permanent, and grow constantly worse, because the nerves and brain are so engorged, and clotted, and ulcerated, and sore, that they will not heal, but only grow worse and more incurable. And, of course, as they grow worse the mild forms of mania become the wildest insanity and incurable madness.

As we shall not have time to finish this argument to-night, let us review, and collect together the principal points thus far developed.

We have found that the brain is a continuation and concentration of the nerves, that reach all over and through the body;

That the brain is the organ of the mind or soul;

That the brain is fed and supplied by the blood, sent from the heart, through the arteries;

an active man to take it out half as fast as we put it in.

Dr. Beaumont used to look into the young man's stomach every day; and continued to do so for more than fourteen years.

And the doctor hired the young man to go with him to Washington City, and to stay with him there, on purpose to try experiments with food and drink in his stomach. The inside of a healthy stomach has a light-pink color, as all doctors well know.

(*See Sewell's Plates, No.* 1.)

And as Alexis St. Martin was a healthy, stout boy, his stomach was pink-colored also, at first. But by and by he got so he liked liquor; and, as he had grown to be a man, the doctor had to let him do as he pleased. After he had been drinking pretty hard for a few days, Dr. Beaumont looked into his stomach, and found it — no longer pink, but fiery red, and very much congested or inflamed. When St. Martin would quit drinking for a few days, the doctor would look in, and find the stomach pink-colored, healthy, and all right again.

Dr. Beaumont wrote a book all about it long ago, before the Temperance Reform began. Out of that book I make this quotation: —

"The free use of ardent spirits, wine, beer, or any of the intoxicating liquors, when continued for some days, has invariably produced those morbid changes in St. Martin's stomach."

Ah! invariably done it. And the doctor made these kind of examinations for fourteen years. Well, that is something; but I have something more. Dr. Thomas Sewell, who was then a young doctor, used to go and look into St. Martin's stomach some-

That the arteries in the lower part of the brain are larger than they are in the upper part, and, therefore, there is more alcohol and corrupt blood acting upon the lower organs, to stimulate or inflame them;

That the organs of thirst, attack, acquisition, amativeness, and other animal organs are located in the lower part of the brain;

That the location of these organs has been abundantly proved by writers on phrenology;

That, when they are injured by alcohol, the person will be apt to be overcome by a mania to drink, mania to injure, mania to kill, mania for suicide, mania to steal, mania to lie, mania to gamble, mania to rob, mania for lust, or some other form of mania;

That when several of these forms of mania are present in the same mind, it is properly called insanity or madness, and is always coupled with depravity;

That the organs which are already large and supported by large arteries are apt to be stimulated the most by the use of alcoholic liquors;

That the keenness and clearness and accuracy of the whole mind or soul are dulled, and blunted and beclouded and depraved and weakened by them;

And that these various forms of mania, insanity, madness, foolishness, and depravity, at first only temporary, frequently become wild, raging, raving, and incurable.

SHALL MANIA PREVAIL?

Shall man, well endowed with a rational mind,
    And wise, beyond all of the creatures of earth,
Judging, perceiving, and loving, refined —
    The image of Him who created the earth,
With conscience, and reason, and hopefulness filled,
    And these all immortal — composing the soul,
With honor enwrapped, and with cheerfulness thrilled,
    And grand as the heavens that over him roll;

ALCOHOL.

Shall he be destroyed, and broken, and crushed,
    And darkly o'erwhelmed with oblivion's cloud,—
His holy emotions all silenced and hushed,
    And covered, and wrapped in so mournful a shroud,
By the demon of drink, who betrays with a kiss,
    And who kills, while pretending to nourish and cheer;
Who robs his poor victims of heaven and bliss,
    And takes from them all that is noble and dear?

Shall mania prevail when the mind should be well;
    And madness succeed over reason dethroned;
Insanity wild, and delirum fell,
    Take possession of him whom the angels have owned?
Shall hate take the place of love in the heart,
    And wickedness dwell where the lovely has been?
Shall endearments be sundered, — torn rudely apart?
    And man given over to passion and sin?

Then banish the fiend from the face of the earth;
    Or kill him at once, for the good of the race?
Drive him hence, from your kindred, your children, and hearth,
    All covered with shame, and all dark with disgrace!
Drive him hence! Drive him hence! and as soon as you can;
    Make him go from the mind where reason once beamed;
Let the poor, despised drunkard, once more be a man;
    Let the soul of the victim be nobly redeemed.

VI

ALCOHOL — WHAT EFFECT HAS IT UPON THE IMMORTAL MIND? — DOES IT EVER CAUSE INDOLENCE, IGNORANCE, OR DEPRAVITY? — IS IT EVER THE CAUSE OF MANIA, INSANITY, MADNESS, LUNACY, DELIRIUM, WICKEDNESS, OR CRIME? — DOES IT INCREASE THE NUMBER OF DOLTS, IDIOTS, AND FOOLS? — IN WHAT WAY? — AND WHY?

VI.

Webster, in his unabridged Dictionary, says that lunacy is "a species of insanity or madness; properly the kind of insanity which is broken by intervals of reason, any unsoundness of mind, derangement, craziness, mania."

And, as this lecture is a continuation of the preceding one, we shall further undertake to show that the use of alcoholic or intoxicating liquors is the great and all-prevailing cause of "unsoundness of mind, derangement, craziness, mania."

Let me tell you, ladies and gentlemen, that there comes a time in the history of the drunkard, when he no longer imagines himself king, nor lord, nor noble; when he forgets to be witty, and has no desire to sing; when he has no desire to lie, nor steal, and no longing for lust; when even his desire to break, and burn, and kill is hushed into silence. The organ of caution becomes inflamed, and he becomes over-cautious and fearful, and trembles with terror. The nerves of the eye become inflamed, and he sees strange and awful sights, wild animals, fierce beasts, slimy and venomous serpents, huge, terrible, and hideous. The nerves of the ear become inflamed, and he hears strange and awful noises, hears the crackling of flames, the growling of monsters, the screeching of fierce birds, the loud laughter of fiends. The nerves of the nose become inflamed, and he smells terrible stenches and smokes. The nerves of feeling become inflamed, and he feels the sharp points of spears, the edges of knives, the claws of dragons, the hot coals and blazes of burning ruins. The nerves of taste become irritated and inflamed, and he tastes bitter herbs, acrid liquors, and fiery drugs. The nerves of imagination become irritated and inflamed, and he imagines sights and sounds more terrible than ever existed in society, and he quakes and gasps with terror. The nerves of memory become inflamed at last, and he recalls the image of a praying mother, a loving and beseeching wife, and the smiles of his innocent children. Anguish and hopeless remorse take possession of his soul; and while he is thus raving and calling for protection against these myriad evils, the vital organs of the body, scorched and burned with alcohol, cease to perform their accustomed duties, and the victim dies. His soul thus bewildered and tortured, passes to the land of spirits, where everlasting silence reigns.

Now, what shall we call this last condition of the drunkard's mind? Delirium? What is delirium? Webster says it is "a state of the mind, in which the ideas of a person are wild, irregular, and unconnected; mental aberration, a raving or wandering of the mind." Thus we have traced the evil effects of intoxicating liquors, from their entrance into the stomach, through a myriad avenues, to the scorching and burning of the brain, and the development of mental delirium.

But perhaps you want other authorities, besides those already mentioned, to estabish the conclusions arrived at in this lecture and the former one.

They are at hand and you shall have them.

From the report of the United States census of 1860, we learn that the "brain is the organ of thought, the machinery through which all the operations of the mind are evolved." And we learn from the same report, that "the use of intoxicating liquors is a very great source of mental derangement." The census is taken by order of the National Government, by able, impartial, and responsible men, and their report is sworn to; and therefore a statement in that report should have great weight in determining a doubtful point.

Dr. Austin Flint, Professor of Physiology in Bellevue Hospital Medical College, in the city of New York, has recently published a very able work on the Principles and Practice of Medicines, from which I quote these words: "The deleterious influence of alcohol on the mental is not less marked than on the physical powers. The inebriate exemplifies a variety of the forms of mental derangement, called dipsomania, from which recovery is extremely rare. The perceptions are blunted, the intellectual and moral faculties progressively deteriorate, until at length the confirmed inebriate, miserably cachetic in body and imbruted in mind, has but one object in life, namely, to gratify the morbid cravings of alcohol." Is not that sound on the temperance question? Dr. Flint's book was not written for a "temperance tract," but a standard work for the medical profession. As such the profession has adopted it.

And now let me refer you to another standard medical author, Dr. M. H. Romberg, of Germany, who was for twenty-eight years a physician in one of the largest union hospitals of Berlin, Prussia, and afterwards for a number of years Director of Clinics in the University of Berlin, and who, during all that time has seen, perhaps, fifty thousand cases of mental disease, and who has written some two thousand pages on the Diseases of the Nerves and Brain, for the medical profession. From his great book we quote:—

"The diseased condition of the blood and its vessels exerts an undoubted influence on the mind. The affections of the mind, such as vertigo, dizziness, fear, terror, etc., are caused in a great measure by the continued use of spirituous liquors and other narcotics, taken into the blood, that inflame the blood-vessels of the nerves and brain." Is that language strong enough, for you? Let me quote again from Dr. Romberg, and I wish you to take particular notice of this, because I shall use it hereafter when we come to consider the adulteration of liquors. It is this: "The most frequent exciting causes of neuralgia, vertigo, and many other nervous diseases, are intoxication by alcoholic liquors, and the use of other narcotics and the organic vegetable alkalies, such as tobacco, belladonna, digitalis, hyoscyamus, stramonium, etc. Alcohol and narcotics act upon the brain and spinal chord. The state of the blood is depraved by these poisons, and it (thus depraved) reacts upon the brain. It affects the nerves of the eye so as to make it see sights that do not exist; and upon the nerves of sound, so as to make them hear sounds that do not exist, such as boiling, screeching, hammering, cutting, etc. After a time the mind becomes clouded, and sopor, and paralysis, and death intervene." Dr. Romberg gives a number of cases that he dissected. One of them was a case of cholera, from intoxication, when, "on making the post-mortem examination, he found the larger veins on the surface of the brain, as well as the blood-vessels in the substance of the brain, engorged with blood." Dr. Romberg was not writing a " temperance tract," but a scientific work for the whole profession. Dr. Munroe says, "The blood, becoming so impaired by the use of alcoholic beverages, is no longer able to sustain the brain in a healthy condition." And he mentions cases of epilepsy and apoplexy, when he made post-mortem examinations, and, on cutting through the congested brain, he discovered a multitude of "minute blood spots (where the arteries had burst), indicating a great amount of pressure in the blood-vessels."

Dr. Cheyne describes a case of a drunken sea-captain, who was struck with paralysis, and died in a few hours. On examination, he found the brain "divided in the middle by quite a puddle of blood."

Dr. John H. Bennett, Professor of Clinical Medicine in the University of Edinburgh, who has written a thousand pages on diseases of the mind, says that "alcohol is a poison which especially affects the nervous system, and more particularly the brain."

Dr. Percy made a number of dissections, where he found the blood-vessels burst, and blood and alcohol mingled with the substance of the brain. Dr. Huss did the same, with the same results. These gentlemen, and many others, found cases where part of the brain had turned to fat, from the presence of alcohol; and a number of cases where part of the brain had decayed, or turned to pus, or matter, from the same cause.

Let me quote also from Dr. John Higginbottom, of the Royal College of Surgeons, whose writings are good authority with doctors everywhere. "Alcohol is particularly destructive to the brain and nervous system, and, consequently, to the mental and physical powers of the whole body. Drunkenness and insanity appear so near akin, that drunkenness has been called voluntary insanity, and we often find that such voluntary insanity terminates in involuntary and incurable insanity."

Dr. E. L. Cleveland says, "At first it sparkles and cheers, and excites mirth and song. But at last it poisons and maddens, and produces sorrow and curses, and feuds, and fighting, and murder, and emasculates the mind of every element of strength, and degrades the conversation to the merest stammering of idiotic gibberish, until the man becomes a dilapidated and vulgar sot, and at last sinks into the slough of despondency and mental horror, until death kindly relieves him of his misery."

Dr. Morel, of France, was for several years connected with Salpetriere Hospital, where there are more than one thousand insane people, and afterwards was for several years Superintendent of Mareville

Lunatic Asylum, where there are more than one thousand more of these poor, demented human beings. After seventeen years of experience he has written a book, and from his book we quote his testimony as follows: "There is always a hopeless number of paralytic and other insane persons in our (French) hospitals, whose disease is due to no other cause than the abuse of alcoholic liquors. In one thousand, upon whom I have made especial observation, not less than two hundred owed their mental disorder to no other cause." What do you think of that? That is in France, where it is supposed they drink "wine only." Two hundred out of a thousand. Which is equal to twenty per cent. For not less than twenty per cent. of the insanity of France, he could find no other cause. Dr. Morel was not writing a work on temperance, and therefore has not told us that thirty per cent. of the other known causes, such as "excessive grief," "disappointed affection," etc., were created by the drinking of alcoholic liquors.

Another learned Frenchman, by the name of Behics, in making a report on the physical causes of insanity in France, says that " of eight thousand and eight hundred male lunatics, and seven thousand and one hundred female lunatics, thirty-four per cent. of the men, and six per cent. of the women were made insane by intemperance. He was not writing a temperance report, and therefore did not include those who became insane from "disappointed ambition," "unrequited love," "loss of property and position," "excessive grief," etc., brought on by the drunkenness of fathers, husbands, and friends, which would swell the thirty-four per cent. to more than fifty per cent., for both male and female. I know at least one case, where a father became insane from excessive grief, because his son became a drunkard. And at the asylum he was registered as insane from excessive grief. A wife went insane because her husband made a drunken beast of himself, squandered her property, and abused her person; and her name was registered as insane from "unhappy domestic relations." A pious sister became insane because her drunken brother — for whom she most earnestly prayed, and with whom she most zealously plead — would not repent of his sins, nor join the church, nor listen to her pleadings, but spurned her from his presence with harsh and bitter oaths. At the asylum her name was registered as insane from "excessive religious zeal." Thus the records cover the real causes with gilded phrases, rather than offend the dignity of besotted relatives.

Motet says that "more than one-fourth of the insane (in France) whose malady is due to physical causes, suffer the penalty of alcoholic excesses. Among eight thousand seven hundred and ninety-seven cases of the insane from physical causes, three thousand and forty-four were drunkards (ivrognes)." These figures represent over thirty per cent., or nearly one-third.

But Motet, like the rest, was not considering the various "domestic troubles" and other exciting causes, that so frequently result from drunkenness in the family, and which, if considered, would swell the number to over fifty per cent. of all the lunatics in the land.

I have not time to-night to quote from Dr. Reuben D. Mussey, of Vermont, but will say this much, that his writings fully and pointedly confirm quite a number of the leading points in this and some of my preceding lectures. His writings are powerful and convincing temperance arguments. I may quote at another time.

Dr. Hiram Cox, a distinguished chemist of Cincinnati, Ohio, acting as a physician to the Probate Court of that city, examined upwards of four hundred cases of insanity, previous to sending them to the State Asylum; and he says that "two-thirds of their number became insane from drinking the poisonous liquors sold at the doggeries and taverns of our city and county.

"Many of them were boys nineteen or twenty years of age, some of whom were laboring under a hereditary taint, — and perhaps in many of them the mental derangement would never have been developed, had they not drank these poisonous decoctions."

Let us listen to the learned Dr. Sewell: "The inebriate first loses his vivacity and natural acuteness of perception. His judgment becomes clouded and impaired in its strength, the memory also enfeebled and sometimes quite obliterated. The mind is wandering and vacant, and incapable of intense or steady application to any one subject.

"Inflammation and engorgement of the brain are frequent consequences of intemperance, and may take place during a debauch, — or may arise some time after, during the stage of debility, from the loss of a healthy balance of action between the different parts of the system. This inflammation is sometimes acute, is marked by furious delirium, and terminates fatally in the course of a few days, and sometimes a few hours. At other times it assumes a chronic form, continues much longer, and then frequently results in an effusion of serum, or an extravasation of blood, and then the patient dies in a state of insensibility, with all the symptoms of compressed brain."

Let me quote from a distinguished and learned philanthropist, who spoke on this subject forty years ago: "The influence on the mind is similar to that which is exerted on the body. Strong drink generates, perhaps, as many mental as physical diseases. The momentary effect of this stimulus is exhilaration. But this state of excitement cannot long continue, and it must be followed by a tremendous intellectual reaction. It is a blazing fire which consumes itself and soon burns out. The discriminating powers are not aided even by the present excitement of spirituous liquor. The imagination may mount on a more lofty pinion, or fancy display a more gaudy plume; but in these very cases the understanding is generally embarrassed, and the judgment grossly perverted. I would not trust a man — I care not what his intellect may be — who is excited by strong drink, in any business which demands cool investigation. The mind is biased, impatient, and unstrung. The powers of discrimination are blunted; the more buoyant faculties soon flag; and the imagination, which was accustomed to soar, soon crawls upon the earth. The immortal mind of the drunkard is not less blighted by this withering curse than his dying body. His memory, once retentive and ready, has lost its wonted power. His understanding, which could once grasp and wield and elucidate almost any subject, becomes debilitated and childish. In his cups the drunkard is generally a temporary madman.

"But idiocy and insanity are not always temporary in the case of the drunkard.

Both of these effects often become permanent in the future man. Idiots may be found almost everywhere, who have brought this calamity upon themselves by the immoderate use of ardent spirits. From men of intellect and men of business, and perhaps men of pre-eminent attainments, they have debased themselves to a common level with the swine. In some cases reason seems to be blotted out, and the miserable victim of intemperance lives and dies a literal fool. In other cases still more numerous, there is a manifest approximation to idiocy, where this deplorable consequence does not actually follow. Who has not witnessed the wane of intellect around him? Who has not seen the shrewd accountant become dull; the profound philosopher rendered obtuse; the arch politician bewildered; the eager flight of the learned advocate flag; and that precocity of genius which, in the dawn of life, attracted the steady gaze, and promised a giant manhood, dwindle into mental insignificance and death? The world may, perhaps, stand and wonder at the change, and speculate upon the latent cause. But lift the curtain, and the mystery is solved. There stands the bottle, and the death of intellect in it. Trace the effects of this habit upon the talents, and learning, and prospects of a young man of early promise; fix your eye upon one who is gifted with as fine a mind as was ever moulded by the hand of Heaven; and let him become addicted to his cups; and let him continue to suck and suck at the bottle, and he will ultimately become a besotted dolt, a mere idiot.

"As to madness, every one knows that it is a common effect of excessive drinking. It is stated on good authority that one-third of all the cases of insanity, in the United States, may be traced to intemperance as the direct cause. Oh, what misery does this poisonous cup inflict! What transformation of those creatures who were made to stand erect, and who were originally formed in the image of God! To be a sensible man, by and by a fool, and presently a beast!"

I wish to refer you now to the report of the Board of State Charities of the Commonwealth of Massachusetts for the year 1866, carefully prepared by seven gentlemen, — three of them physicians — as drawn up by Dr. Nathan Allen, of Lowell. I quote the following : —

"It is well known that alcohol stimulates the lower propensities and weakens the higher faculties. Everybody knows that a certain dose acts upon certain faculties so as to make a man jolly, while a greater, acts upon other faculties, so as to make him quarrelsome and angry.

"Alcohol, taken into the stomach or absorbed in the skin, must mingle, undigested, with the blood; and alcoholized blood stimulates the blood in a peculiar manner. A large dose stimulates those organs or functions which manifest themselves in what we call propensities or animal passions, and represses those organs or functions which manifest themselves in the higher or human sentiments, which result in (refinement, morality, and) will. If the blood, thus highly alcoholized, goes to the brain, its functions become subverted; the man does not know and does not care what he says or does. If this process is often repeated, the lower propensities are strengthened by exercise, until, by and by, they act of their own accord, while the restraining (moral) powers or will, weakened by disease, are practically nullified. The man is no longer under the control of his voluntary power, but is under the dominion of his lower organs, and they (the lower organs) are almost as much beyond his control, as the beating of his heart. The habitual stimulus of the brain by alcoholized blood — in ever so small doses — must produce the same kind of result, only in a lesser degree. Blood that is alcoholized, must have this peculiar effect upon the brain, namely, to excite and intensify the lower propensities, and to lessen (and weaken) the voluntary and restraining powers. It excites the animal nature to powerful and ungovernable activity, and utterly paralyzes (judgment) reason, conscience, and will."

So says Dr. Allen. So say we all.

According to the United States census, we have in the republic about twenty-four thousand insane people. And we have already shown that one-half of this number become so from intoxicating drink. Twelve thousand victims to insanity! Twelve thousand raving maniacs, from this evil alone! And this continually. One-third of them die every year, and new ones come to fill their places. Three thousand a year cast into the awful vortex of death from madness, from this one vice alone! Three thousand annually, go — raving and distracted — into the jaws of death!

The remaining two-thirds are cured, after three years of treatment, at great expense; and are returned to their homes, shattered and broken-down relics of their former selves. Their bodies wrecked; their minds in ruins; ghastly shadows of departed worth.

Once more. And now we come to the idiots. An idiot is one who lacks ordinary sense; one who is deficient in mental ability, — wanting in some of the common faculties of the mind; one who lacks capacity or ability to acquire ordinary intelligence; a simpleton; a natural fool.

Webster says, a fool is "one who is destitute of reason, or the common powers of understanding; a person deficient in intellect; an idiot; a simpleton; a dunce; a dolt." The United States census reports about twenty thousand idiots or fools; but this is perhaps, an under estimate, as many parents hate to tell the census officers that their children are fools; for which reason many are reported as sound in mind who are really idiotic. The number of idiots, in most countries, and all ages, has been equal to or greater than the number of insane. Therefore we may safely say that there are twenty-four thousand fools in the United States. And then leave out a host of people who exhibit strong marks of idiocy. The fool-killers have been lenient! The fools are not all dead! Many a man thinks he is wonderfully smart, who is in reality, a fool. I have seen several myself, within a month. It is the easiest thing in the world to be a fool, and not know it!

As already shown in this lecture, drinking is one great cause of idiocy.

Many a man of fine talents has drank himself into a fool. Many a bright boy and man of talent has become a fool while becoming a sot.

And right here I wish to call your attention to a law of human life; namely, the law that "like begets like." Children are like their parents. When we plant acorns, we raise oaks, not hickories. When wheat is sown, it produces wheat, not corn. Weeds produce weeds. Black children come from black parents; diseased children from diseased parents.

"Traits of character, dispositions, aspirations, talents, propensities, passions, depraved conditions and diseases, may be inherited, as well as form, looks, and complexion."

The law that children inherit the traits, weaknesses, and diseases of their parents, is so universally acknowledged by medical men, and so well understood by most intelligent people, that I will not undertake to prove it in this lecture; but refer those who doubt the truth of it to almost any medical book they choose to pick up, and especially to the article on "idiocy" in the Eighth Census. In that report will be found abundant proof, and reference to many able medical writers. It is as old as the days of Aristotle; and as true as the multiplication table. Fowler has thoroughly explained it in his works on Love and Parentage, Matrimony, and Hereditary Descent.

Dr. Carpenter, in his book, quotes from

Dr. Brown, of the Crichton Lunatic Asylum, who says: "The drunkard not only injures and enfeebles his own nervous system, but entails mental disease upon his family. His children are nervous, weak, wayward, and eccentric, and become insane under the pressure of excitement from some unforeseen exigency, or the ordinary calls of duty."

And, referring to his own private practice, he says, "At present I have two patients who appear to inherit a tendency to an unhealthy action of the brain, from mothers addicted to drinking."

Dr. S. G. Howe, in his Report to the Legislature of Massachusetts, makes the following statement: "The habits of the parents of three hundred of the idiots were learned; and one hundred and forty-five — nearly one-half — are reported as known to be habitual drunkards."

This, remember, is in addition to the large

number who started in life with sound minds, but who became idiots through the use of drink. Adding the two together, we become satisfied that more than half of all the idiots in the land become so from their own and their parents' and grandparents' drunkenness!

"The sins of the parents are visited upon the children, to the third and fourth generation." "The parents eat sour grapes, and the children's teeth are set on edge." Woe unto the children of drunkards!

Let me quote again from Dr. Allen's Report: "Every thoughtful man admits the existence of a strong tendency to the hereditary descent, of all conditions and peculiarities of body (and mind), and also that many of these conditions are purely the result of habit. Any morbid condition of the body (or mind), frequently repeated, becomes established by habit. Once established, it affects the man in various ways, and makes him more liable to certain diseases, such as gout, scrofula, insanity, and the like. This liability or tendency he transmits to his children, just as surely as he transmits likeness in form or feature. Now the use of alcohol certainly does induce a morbid condition of the body (and mind). A given dose excites the animal nature to powerful and ungovernable activity, and utterly paralyzes reason, conscience, and the will. But a small dose does the same thing, only in a lesser degree. It is morally certain, therefore, that the frequent or habitual overthrow of the conscience and will, or the habitual weakening of them, soon establishes a morbid condition, with morbid appetites and tendencies, and that these appetites and tendencies are surely transmitted to offspring."

No logic will be able to overthrow that

position. Nothing truer was ever penned by man.

I know of a family of seven children, one of which is a fool. He is now more than twenty years of age, and does not know enough to put on or take off his own clothes. They clothe him in a loose frock, like a woman's dress, and he goes about astride of a stick, with a switch in his hand, like a little boy of four years old, playing horse. He knows how to swear; but that is all he knows of language. A few words will explain it all. Both parents were beastly drunk at the time of conception! They quit drinking; and the other six children have inherited about average intellect.

I know of another family, where the first child has average common sense; the second is very much demented; and the third is a slobbering, drooling fool.

The explanation is easy. After marriage

the parents began drinking, and in six years had become perfect sots.

They have become so diseased and depraved that they can bring forth no more. God Almighty has set a limit to such shameless debauchery. They have cursed the earth with these; but there they have to stop.

Young man, how would you like to be the father of a fool? Or a whole family of fools? If I ask you to show me your children, you point to a litter of idiots, and say, "There, that is the best I could do!" If you do not wish to be the father of fools, then let liquor alone. And if you do not let it alone, the chances are, that you will become a fool yourself; and your posterity after you. Shame, shame upon you!

Young lady, how would you like to be the mother of a family of fools? Then keep clear of a drunken husband! If a young man comes to you who drinks, and thus depraves himself, spurn him from your presence as you would a loathsome leper. He is unclean, — unfit to be the companion of a true woman. If you marry a man, and he afterwards makes a sot of himself, divorce him, — go from his loathsome presence as you would from a filthy beast. Do not permit yourself to be the mother of fools.

Let me quote from Dr. H. R. Storer and Dr. Albert Day, the former of Berkshire Medical College, and the latter of the Inebriate Asylum, Binghampton, New York. They unite in saying that "Epilepsy, idiocy, and insanity, whether noticed at birth, or whether developed later in life, — with or without any exciting cause, — are among the direful effects, so often seen by medical men, in the persons of the children of those who are addicted to habits of intoxication."

Hear that! What an awful warning! They speak of "idiocy, insanity," and other filthy diseases, as being "deliberately entailed, by besotted parents, upon their innocent descendants."

Drunken parents thus make a filthy mockery of human life, and when they die leave only poor, demented, slobbering, dirty, half-witted representatives behind them. Shame, shame!

These physicians further say, "It is not merely the man or woman inflamed by alcohol — at or near the time of sexual intercourse — that implants the fatal disease in the child at the very moment of conception; not this and these only; but they are equally guilty, perhaps more so, who, — with their blood diseased from long saturation with this poison, their nervous system shattered, and the very foundations of their being tainted, — proceed deliberately to engender offspring."

Like begets like; their children will be like themselves. Woe unto the children of drunkards!

There are exceptions, of course; but this is the usual rule. No intelligent man will deny it. Thus we account for over one-half of all the idiots. Twelve thousand idiots curse the land, from drunken parents! Is liquor a curse? Or is it not? Add to this number twice twelve thousand more, who are almost idiots, — just a shade above the fool, and many of them otherwise diseased, — and you have a sickening, but truthful, picture of the awful ravages of the liquor scourge.

Webster defines wickedness to be "evil in principle or practice; contrary to the moral law; evil disposition, or practice; immorality; crime; sin; sinfulness."

And this brings us to consider the last and most heart-revolting topic of all, crime; crime against the property and persons of others, which is largely caused by the demon, drink. In my Lecture No. 5 I have shown the reasons why it causes crime. In this one let me specify a little more fully. And what is crime? Webster says it is "any violation of law, whether divine or human; an omission of a duty which is commanded, or the commission of an act which is forbidden by law; violation of law; gross offence."

Among the milder forms of the drunkard's crimes, perhaps, is the neglecting of his business, the wasting of his time, the squandering of his money, and annoying decent society by his filthy, noisy presence.

A drunkard comes into your shop, or store, or house, and although he may not be violent, he bores you out of your time, or frightens your wife or children, or dirties up your furniture and room, or disgusts you with his indecent, filthy, lying gibberish, and you long to have him gone.

Then come theft, and cruelty to animals, and the losing, breaking, and burning of property. Then follow assault and battery, and riot, resulting in personal injury, or rape, or robbery, or murder, or all combined; for the drunken brutes scarcely know the crimes they commit. Does the drinking of liquor cause people to commit any of these crimes, or does it not? The man who says it does not, knows that he is himself a liar.

The chaplain of the Massachusetts State Prison inquired into the causes of crimes, and testifies that nineteen out of every twenty, confined within those prison walls, were there for crimes committed through the agency of liquor; and nearly all of them while actually under the immediate influence of liquor.

Out of twenty-two murders, twenty were committed while under the maddening influence of intoxicating spirits.

Lieutenant Governor Trask had before him six hundred applications for pardon for criminals confined in prison, all but two of whom committed their crimes while under the influence of liquor.

And this only confirms the opinion, long since expressed, of eminent men, who have spent their lives in the court-room.

Listen to some of the judges in the court of Great Britain. I quote from Mr. Delavan: —

JUDGE COLERIDGE: "There is scarcely a crime comes before me that is not, directly or indirectly, caused by strong drink."

JUDGE GURNEY: "Every crime has its origin, more or less, in drunkenness."

JUDGE PATTERSON: "If it were not for this drinking, you (the jury) and I would have nothing to do."

JUDGE ANDERSON: "Drunkenness is the most fertile source of crime; and if it could be removed, the assizes of the country would be rendered mere nullities."

JUDGE WIGHTMAN: "I find in every calendar that comes before me, one unfailing source, directly or indirectly, of most of the crimes that are committed, — intemperance."

Lord Acton, Supreme Judge of Rome, declared that "nearly all the crimes of Rome originate in the use of wine."

Many lawyers, judges, and statesmen, in our own country, have expressed similar opinions. And these opinions are shared by Rev. Messrs. Miner, Beecher, Chapin, and other clergymen.

In our own city of Chicago, during the

year 1867, there were twenty-three thousand arrests. And more than twenty thousand of them were brought about by the agency of intoxication.

Intoxication, therefore, is the infernal source, from which flows the black and filthy stream of crime. Drunkenness is the filthy nest in which depravity, shame, and wickedness are hatched, and from which the hellish brood of crime crawls forth. Alcohol is the father of four-fifths of all the crimes, whether small or great.

There were about six hundred cases of suicide in the United States during the year 1867. During the same time there were about eight hundred murders; fifteen hundred rapes; five thousand robberies; five thousand cases of arson; one hundred thousand cases of larceny and theft; besides a countless host of small, petty crimes and misdemeanors.

Four-fifths of all these crimes are chargeable to the use of liquors. To this must be added four-fifths of all the cost of detection and punishment. And even this does not complete the bill of indictment against intoxication.

Four-fifths of all the accidents that happen, by land and sea, are chargeable to the same cause, through its effect upon the body and mind of man.

The cars run off the track, because the engineer has been drinking; a bridge or a building falls, because the builder, being under the influence of liquor at the time, failed to build it well; and a steamship, in mid-ocean, is set on fire by the carelessness of a tipsy hand, and burns to the water's edge.

Even this does not complete the bill. The blighting scourge of poverty sweeps over half a million families, leaving gaunt hunger and ghastly want in its desolate track, from the drunkenness and debauchery of husbands and fathers.

Nor can we begin to estimate the awful magnitude of the evil until we begin to add together and sum up the items, to find its great and calamitous results.

The myriad forms of mania; the wide and deep cesspool of vulgar blasphemy and sin; the wild horrors of delirium; the nameless mingling of mental diseases and temporary insanity, until permanent insanity is reached, and twelve thousand raving maniacs are thrown into the awful vortex, and twice twelve thousand more, shattered, ruined minds, wrecked and stranded by insanity, and even yet *almost* insane; and this awful collection, followed by twelve thousand slobbering idiots, and twice twelve thousand more, poor, demented creatures, just a little above idiocy, and fifty thousand more, who are not idiots, but whose minds are much inferior to what they might have been; and these followed by the awful catalogue of crimes, all the way from petty theft and petty assaults up to manslaughter and murder; and these horrors followed by the stupendous cost of taking care of these unfortunate wretches; and these again followed by startling calamities and accidents that curdle and clog the current of one's blood; and, finally, all of these overshadowed and darkened by the frowning pall of poverty and want. Few minds are able to comprehend the awful magnitude of the alcoholic horror. Meekly and modestly we bow to the All-Wise Father of Mankind, whose mercy endures forever, and beseechingly implore his all-directing aid.

And be pleased to remember that, in making up these conclusions, we have not depended wholly on our own investigations, but have quoted from Drs. Gall, Spurzheim, Combe, Fowler, Gray, Brinton, Flint, Romberg, Munroe, Cheyne, Bennett, Percy, Huss, Higginbottom, Cleveland, Morel, Behics, Motet, Mussey, Cox, Sewell, Kerk, Allen, Brown, Howe, Storer, Day, and the eminent physicians who prepared the medical articles for the eighth census; and, besides these, have quoted from lawyers, statesmen, judges, and clergymen.

Do you doubt the conclusions? If so, then investigation is in vain, and argument is folly. I leave the decision of this cause to the people, and to posterity.

VII.

Alcohol — How much is made? — How many Factories? — How much Grain and Fruit is used in making it? — How many People are thus employed? — In how many Places is it kept for Sale? — How many People drink it? — How soon do the Victims die? — How many Years of human Life are wasted? — How great is the Number of the Dead? — How many Drinkers are reformed? — And Who?

VII.

HAVING already ascertained the nature of alcohol; having already shown its baneful effects upon the human body; having already traced the appalling injuries inflicted, all along its journey through the immortal mind; having demonstrated the manner in which it curses the body with loathsome diseases, and makes a shattered wreck of the ever-living soul; having pointed out the manner in which it injures society, and lays its leprous hand upon the human race, — my duty as a faithful citizen of the great republic requires me to measure the quantity that is made and used, and number the people who are making, selling, and consuming it, — to estimate its magnitude as an article of trade and commerce, and measure its ruinous influence upon the nation.

The task is a great one, and were it not a duty, I should gladly leave it to other hands. He who shrinks from duty, — he who is able to benefit his race by exposing a dangerous foe, and does not do it, is unworthy of himself, — unworthy of the name of man.

I have compiled, from the reports of the United States revenue officers, from the late census tables of the republic, from the census reports of a number of cities, from the health reports of cities, asylums, and hospitals, and other reliable sources, that cannot fail to be of some value to the people.

I have taken the liberty to strike out the fractions, so as to present the facts in whole numbers; and in a few instances, where the reports were not sufficiently definite or complete, to make estimates, from the partial tables on hand, so as to leave out the mass of details, and the multitude of particulars, and present only the prominent facts and features that are of general interest to all the people.

During the year 1867 there was made in the United States about one hundred million gallons of distilled spirits, — equal to three gallons to every man, woman, and child in the whole republic!

Now, as one bushel of grain, or its equivalent in sugar or starch (see Lectures No. 1 and 2), will only make about four gallons of common whiskey, it follows that the manufacturing of distilled spirits during the year consumed twenty-five million bushels of grain.

The city of Chicago alone, with her twenty-five distilleries, made two million gallons of distilled liquors, and used up half a million bushels of grain in doing so. And, as the population of Chicago is only a quarter of a million, it follows that the liquors made here would supply eight gallons to every living soul in the corporation, and used up two bushels of grain from each and every inhabitant. If every other community were as industrious in this line of business as the city of Chicago, the total number of gallons of distilled liquors would be three times one hundred million gallons. But we always expect Chicago to be a little ahead in everything.

These one hundred million gallons of distilled liquors were made in fifteen hundred distilleries, scattered all over the land, but chiefly in the grain and sugar producing sections of the country. For sugar, you remember, or starch, which is convertible into sugar, is the substance out of which alcohol is made. Counting ten men to each distillery (not counting, at present, those indirectly employed), there were fifteen thousand men directly employed in distilling liquors.

During the same time there were made in the United States four hundred million gallons of brewed liquors, — beer, ale, and porter, — equal to twelve gallons to each and every soul in the great republic!

And since one bushel of grain will make about twenty gallons of beer, it follows, that, in brewing these liquors, twenty million bushels of grain were used.

Here, again, Chicago is a little ahead; for her forty breweries made, in 1867, eight million gallons of beer and ale, — equal to thirty-two gallons to each and every one of her inhabitants; and used up four hundred thousand bushels of grain, — equal to nearly two bushels of grain to each inhabitant.

But our breweries — like our gentlemen

and our ladies — are more numerous, perhaps, and larger than they are in any other community.

Adding the grain that was distilled to the grain that was brewed, in our city, and we have nearly four bushels to each inhabitant, counting all ages and colors.

This vast ocean of brewed liquors, amounting to four hundred million gallons in the United States, was made in three thousand breweries, and, allowing five men to each brewery, employed directly about fifteen thousand men.

Besides these two great varieties and modes of producing liquors, — distilling and brewing, — there is the third, in commercial importance, the wine-making interest. Wines, you will remember, are made by fermenting the sweet juices of various fruits, — such as grapes, apples, peaches, and berries; and various vegetables, — such as rhubarb, potatoes, and beets. There were made in our country, during the year 1867, about twenty million gallons of wine. This consumed nearly ten million bushels of fruits,— the sweetest, nicest, and most delicious fruits of the whole country.

To make these twenty million gallons of wine required the labor, direct, of about ten thousand men.

In addition to these three great sources of intoxicating liquors, there is still another, — importation. While all these distilleries and breweries were busily engaged in making and all these wine (and cider) vats were fermenting, many ships and steamers were also importing liquors from foreign lands. They brought over, in 1867, of all varieties, about twenty million gallons. To make these foreign liquors, there were consumed, beyond the sea, about seven million bushels of grains, fruits, and vegetables, and required the labor of about ten thousand men.

Now let us use a little plain arithmetic, and see what the sum of all these liquors looks like : —

QUANTITY OF LIQUORS MADE.

Distilled liquors, . . .	100,000,000 gallons.
Brewed liquors, . . .	400,000,000 "
Wines (fermented juices),	20,000,000 "
Imported liquors, . . .	20,000,000 "
Total, . . .	540,000,000 "

There is enough to float a respectable navy. And the grains, fruits, and vegetables consumed in making these various liquors, were as follows : —

QUANTITY OF GRAINS AND FRUITS CONSUMED.

Distilled into whiskey, etc.,	25,000,000 bushels.
Brewed into beer, etc., .	20,000,000 "
Fermented into wine, etc.,	10,000,000 "
In imported liquors, . .	7,000,000 "
Total,	62,000,000 "

That is, two bushels to each and every living soul in the entire nation. No wonder provisions are high, and many people are hungry.

Now, as "alcohol is the intoxicating ingredient" in all these liquors (that are not adulterated with other poisons), and since all that part of them which is not alcohol is water, slop, or swill of an inferior grade, let us ascertain the amount of pure alcohol (supposing that none of them were adulterated with other instant poisons before leaving the factory) contained in them.

Since distilled spirits are about half alcohol (see Lectures No. 1 and 2), brewed spirits about seven per cent. alcohol, and wines about twenty-one per cent. alcohol, it follows that there was made as follows:—

QUANTITY OF PURE ALCOHOL MADE.

In distilled spirits, . . . 50,000,000 gallons.
In brewed spirits, . . . 28,000,000 "

In fermented spirits (wine), 4,200,000 gallons.
In imported spirits, . . 4,800,000 "
Total, . . 87,000,000 "

Which is two and a half gallons of alcohol for every man, woman, and child that lives in the whole of our beautiful land.

If there is a man in this nation whose mind is not blunted by this pestilence, whose morals are not polluted by contamination, and whose body is not diseased and besotted, and who loves his kindred and his race, let him hear and ponder; and then, when he has heard and reflected, let him act as becomes a man. There is a God in heaven; let not the day of light and justice be too long postponed on earth. The children of men are hoping, longing, waiting, for that happy day. When? Oh, when?

Since the balance left, after deducting

ITS NATURE AND EFFECTS. 281

the pure alcohol, is only water and inferior slop, let us ascertain the

QUANTITY OF SLOP MADE AND MIXED.

Distilled water,	50,000,000	gallons.
Brewed slops,	372,000,000	"
Fermented slops,	15,800,000	"
Foreign slops,	15,200,000	"
Total,	453,000,000	"

Which is eleven gallons of slop to every man, woman, and child. As we don't all drink, somebody must drink more than eleven gallons a year. No, I thank you! I believe I would rather not. A "peck of dirt" in a lifetime is enough. I prefer not to mix any fermented slop in my dirt.

There are, in the United States, about six thousand wholesale establishments where these various liquors are sold by the quantity. Five men to each establishment would make thirty thousand men engaged in the wholesale trade.

We have one hundred and twenty-five wholesale liquor-houses in Chicago alone. We have nearly that number of churches. But five men are on duty in each of the wholesale liquor-houses six days in a week; while only one man is on duty in each church, a small part of one day in each week. Thirty days' labor against one is hardly fair. Does the world move? Or is there a dead-lock in things generally? Or are we crawfishes, progressing backwards?

There are, in the republic, about one hundred and ten thousand saloons, restaurants, hotels, and stores (not counting drug-stores), and steamboats, where alcoholic liquors are sold at retail, in which two hundred and fifty thousand men and five thousand women are engaged. Dividing these saloons between thirty-two million people, it gives one saloon to every three hundred inhabitants. In the country districts and smaller villages there are only about half this number, which is one saloon to every six hundred people; but in the larger cities about twice this average number, which is one saloon to every one hundred and fifty people.

I am inclined to think these figures are all too low. You will readily see that they are too low in our own city of Chicago. Here there are about two thousand places where liquor is sold at retail to a population of two hundred and fifty thousand people; which is equal to one saloon to every one hundred and twenty-five people, — one to every thirty-five male adults instead of every one hundred and twenty-five people.

But Chicago is, perhaps, an exception (though I do not think it is), — a liquor drinker's Canaan, — a sort of a drunkard's Paradise! Can it be that the day is coming in the misty future when another Milton, pure-souled and brilliant, shall tune his all-bewailing harp, and sing, in martial and mournful numbers, the awful crimes, combats, and misfortunes of another "Paradise Lost"? Let us hope not. Let us hope that the good people of this prosperous and productive region, who believe in the principles of health and temperance, and who take pride in the elevation of the human race, will be able to compose the other part of the immortal epic, and sing, in triumphant numbers, of a "Paradise Regained"!

Let me say that nearly all these figures are rather under-estimates, and will fall short of the actual facts, all the fractions having been struck off in favor of the liquor interest, making it less in magnitude than it really is.

Let us figure up the number of men directly engaged in making and selling:—

ITS NATURE AND EFFECTS. 285

Making distilled liquors,	. . .	15,000 men.
" brewed "	. . .	15,000 "
" wines (fermented),	. .	10,000 "
" foreign liquors,	. . .	10,000 "
Wholesale trade,	. . . . . .	30,000 "
Retail "	. . . . . .	255,000 "
Total,	. . . . . .	335,000 "

How long shall this number of men remain our masters?

Then, one hundred and ten thousand saloons and restaurants are patronized by about four million two hundred thousand people, which is thirteen per cent. of all the people, including women and children. This estimate, like the others, is rather too small; but is sufficiently large to startle a people who call themselves sober, intelligent, and moral.

The four million two hundred thousand people who patronize the saloons may be divided into classes about as follows:—

LIQUOR DRINKERS OR INTEMPERATE PEOPLE.

MALES.

Tasters, or occasional smilers, ... 2,000,000
Moderate drinkers, tipplers, or guzzlers, . 1,500,000
Hard drinkers, inebriates, or regular topers, 300,000
Drunken sots, besotted bloats, or regular old
    tubs, ... 200,000
    Total, ... 4,000,000

FEMALES.

Tasters, or occasional smilers, ... 100,000
Moderate drinkers, tipplers, or guzzlers, . 75,000
Hard drinkers, inebriates, or regular topers, 15,000
Drunken sots, besotted bloats, or regular old
    tubs, ... 100,00
    Total, ... 200,000
Making a grand total of, ... 4200,000

Which is one-seventh of all the people in the whole republic.

In this country one-half of the entire number of people are children, under age. Now, if we deduct sixteen million children from our whole population of thirty-two million, it leaves sixteen million adults, which is about eight million men and eight million women.

As already shown, we have four million male drinkers, which is one-half of all the male adults in the nation; and two hundred thousand female drinkers, which is one-fortieth of all the adult females in the nation.

The annual table of mortality, which follows close behind the drunkenness of the people, arranges itself about as follows: —

MALES.

Suicides, resulting from the use of liquor, . . 350
Deaths from delirium tremens, ... 570
Murders, resulting from the use of liquor, . . 530
Deaths from mania, madness, and insanity,
   from drinking, ... 3,700
Deaths from paralysis, palsy, apoplexy, and
   other diseases of the nerves and brain, including accidents, arising from excited and
   bewildered mind, clearly traceable to the

agency of alcoholic liquors, — and their poisonous compounds — as being the cause, or principal cause of the same, ... 5,000

Deaths from liver, kidney, stomach, bowels, heart, and other diseases of the body, clearly traceable to the agency of alcoholic liquors, and the poisonous adulterations of them, as being the cause, or the principal cause of the same, ... 60,800

Total deaths, males, ... 71,000

FEMALES.

Suicides, resulting from the use of liquors, . . 50

Deaths from delirium tremens, ... 30

Murders, resulting from the use of liquors, . . 20

Deaths from mania, madness, and insanity, from the use of liquors, ... 300

Deaths from paralysis, palsy, apoplexy, and other diseases of the nerves and brain, including accidents arising from excited and bewildered mind, clearly traceable to the agency of alcoholic liquors, and their poisonous compounds, as being the cause, or principal cause of the same, ... 400

Deaths from liver, kidney, stomach, bowels, heart, and other diseases of body, clearly traceable to the agency of alcoholic liquors, and the poisonous adulterations of the same, as being the cause, or principal cause of the same, ... 3,200

Total deaths, females,. 4,000

Remember that Dr. Thomas Sewell, of Washington, says that "Time would fail me, were I to attempt an account of half the pathology of drunkenness. Dyspepsia, jaundice, emaciation, corpulence, dropsy, ulcers, rheumatism, gout, tremors, palpitation, hysteria, epilepsy, palsy, lethargy, apoplexy, melancholy, madness, delirium tremens, and premature old age, compose but a small part of the catalogue of diseases produced by alcoholic drinks. Indeed, there is scarcely a morbid affection to which the human body is liable, that has not, in one way or another, been produced by them. There is not a disease but what they have aggravated, nor a predisposition to disease which they have not called into action."

And remember, also, that Dr. Austin Flint, of Bellevue Hospital Medical College, New York city, in his great work on "The Principles and Practice of Medicine," now used by the profession everywhere, says: "In cases of chronic alcoholism, the digestive powers are weakened, the appetite is impaired, the muscular system is enfeebled, the generative function decays, the blood is impoverished, and the nutrition is imperfect and diseased, as shown by the flabbiness of the skin and muscle, and emaciation or abnormal accumulation of fat. The effects of alcohol enter directly into the causation of many affections, such as cirrhosis of the liver, fatty liver, epilepsy, muscular tremor, gastritis, pyrosis, various dyspeptic disorders, and various lesions of the kidneys. Incidentally, alcohol favors the production of nearly all diseases, by lessening the power of resisting their causes, and contributes to their fatality, by impairing the inability to tolerate and overcome them. Physicians, in these cases, are sometimes bound by delicacy and by prudential considerations to refrain from stating the causes." Thus we are told by our teachers in medicine.

And be pleased not to forget that there is no well-informed and respectable physician in all this land who will undertake to disprove or deny the foregoing statements of Dr. Sewell and Dr. Flint. (See Lectures No. 3 and 4.) They are as well established as the facts that heat, applied to water, creates steam, and that steam can be used as a motive-power.

Now, by adding together the number of deaths, which annually follow the drunkenness of both sexes, we have:—

Suicides from drunkenness,	400
Delirium tremens,	600
Murders from drunkenness,	600
Deaths from insanity, from drunkenness,	3,000
From other diseases of the nerves and brain,	5,400
From diseases of the body, from the same,	65,000
Total number of deaths from drunkenness,	75,000

Which is more than two thousand out of every million people every year.

So far, in this table of mortality, we have not taken into account the wives, sisters, and mothers, who die from grief, from neglect, and from abuse, through the agency of drunken husbands, drunken brothers, and drunken sons, which would swell the number of deaths far beyond seventy-five thousand. But we have only considered those who have themselves used intoxicating liquors to their own great and serious injury, — so much so as to invite and exagerate other diseases, and become the main agents in causing death.

Since the number of deaths among women is about equal to that among men, it follows that the women who die heart-broken with grief and shame, brooding over long neglect and unaccustomed toil, and abused by those who should love and protect them, fighting in the unequal contest against hunger, cold, and want, must be nearly equal to the number of males who kill themselves with drunkenness. If these were counted among the victims of intoxication, — and why should they not be counted, — it would swell the number to more than one hundred thousand, nearly equal to the number of wholesale and retail liquor-shops! The great rebellion, with all its battle-fields and dungeons, did not equal this.

In the normal condition of man, the births exceed the deaths a little, and the race increases. It takes war, pestilence, famine, or vice, to make them equal, and stop its increase.

The annual mortality list for the whole republic, from all diseases and causes, of both sexes and all ages, is now a little less than eight hundred thousand. And we have just shown that over seventy-five thousand deaths are caused, or very much hastened, every year, from intoxicating liquors, which is ten per cent. of all the deaths in the whole republic.

But nearly or quite one-half of all the deaths are of children before they are five years old, which is four hundred thousand. And nearly, or quite, seventy-five thousand children die between the ages of five and fifteen. It is true, that many children, neglected or abused by drunken parents, or who inherited great weaknesses from drunken parents, die earlier than they other-

ITS NATURE AND EFFECTS. 295

wise would; and it is true that many children die between the ages of fifteen and twenty-one; but, without taking either of these facts into consideration at present, we deduct the mortality of four hundred and seventy-five thousand children from the whole number of deaths, and it leaves us a mortality of three hundred and twenty-five thousand adults. And the seventy-five thousand who perish, directly and indirectly, through the agency of alcoholic liquors, fermented, brewed, and distilled, is about twenty-five per cent. of all the deaths of grown-up people. If we add the poor, unfortunate women and children who never drank a drop, but who die victims to drunkenness in others, it would be at least thirty-three per cent. of all adults, or fifteen per cent. of the deaths of all who die.

From these figures, we see that the drinking class of community, the tasters, moderate drinkers, hard drinkers, and drunken sots, all combined, constitute about fifty per cent. of all the adult male population, and nearly two and a half per cent. of the adult females of our land. Not a majority, however.

Let us notice another fact. Nearly all the deaths from delirium tremens, and other mental diseases, and a large share of the worst (alcoholic) physical diseases, come from the class of drunken sots, which diminishes their number at the rate of twenty-five per cent. per annum. This shows that the average duration of a man's life, after he becomes a regular besotted bloat, is only about four years.

When one of these dies, his place is filled from the class of hard drinkers, or inebriates. And this recruiting process, from the one class to the other, goes on at the rate of about fifty thousand per annum. At this rate of depletion, and its own losses added, the class of hard drinkers will exhaust itself in about four years.

And the class of hard drinkers must be replenished from the class of moderate drinkers. And in doing so it will exhaust itself, including its own losses, meanwhile, in about four years. And the class of moderate drinkers must be replenished from the tasters; and, indirectly, from this class all the others are recruited. If there were no tasters, all the other grades and degrees of drinkers would soon perish, and cease to exist.

Now, after deducting the way-side losses, while passing from one grade to another, we find that the average life of a drinking man, after he has fairly become a moderate drinker, is only about ten years.

But, in the ordinary course of nature, all those who pass the age of twenty years should live to the age of sixty years, or a little more.

How does this fact tally with what we have just shown? If a man becomes a moderate drinker at the age of thirty, he drinks himself to death by the time he is forty, and dies twenty years before his time. Some become moderate, but regular drinkers, at twenty, and die of drunkenness at thirty, which is thirty years before their allotted time. Thus they wickedly throw away the last and best half of their lives.

A young man recently died in this city of delirium tremens, who was only twenty-two years old. And another one, not many weeks before him, died of delirium tremens at the age of nineteen. There is a large number of young men in this city, between the ages of seventeen and twenty, who are regular drunkards, and who spend all their wages for drink. There are a good many boys working in the various shops of the city, who spend nearly all their earnings for beer, and are drunk every Saturday night. And some boys, who earn no money themselves, are spending their fathers' money for beer and wine, and bringing shame upon their fathers' memory.

Boys who drink thus at fifteen can hardly reach thirty, and will probably not reach twenty-five years. They will die some shameful death long before they reach their prime.

A few drunkards manage to retain their hold on life for many years; but such ones were fortunate in having a first-class constitution to start on, fortunate in living an active or out-door life, and fortunate in getting liquors with less than the average number of extra foreign poisons in them.

But perhaps the average number of years lost to the man who has once become a moderate but regular drinker is twenty. And these twenty years thus thrown away are taken from the later and most valuable part of his life. Shame, shame upon those who can apologize for and encourage such a reckless waste of human life!

But men waste time with drink before they die. First their evenings, and then their holidays, and then their Sundays, and then their week-days. In the course of the ten years they are drinking their lives away, they waste perhaps two years of time. Waste two years of industry, and then die twenty years too soon; making a total loss of twenty-two years.

If the people only knew the facts as set forth and proved in this course of lectures, nine-tenths of all the tasters, and seven-tenths of all the moderate drinkers would sign the pledge, and shun this black array of evils.

But the people are ignorant. These facts are never spread before them in any responsible manner; and they do not know the awful doom that hangs over them!

There is no society strong enough to print and circulate these facts among the people! Why cannot the temperance people consolidate into one society, so as to print the books and educate the people? While you hesitate to unite, the people perish. "While Rome debated, Saguntum fell!"

Reformation among those who sign the pledge, and join temperance societies or churches, in each of these various classes of drinking people, can be relied upon about as follows, in keeping their pledges, promises, and vows: —

Of the Tasters,	about 75 per ct. are faithful.
" Moderate Drinkers,	" 40	"	"	"
" Hard Drinkers,	" 5	"	"	"
" Drunken Sots,	" 1	"	"	"

Since there are about four thousand five hundred liquor factions, and one hundred and sixteen thousand wholesale and retail liquor-shops in the nation, and something over seventy-five thousand deaths from the liquors therein sold, therefore, if the number of women and children could be taken into account, who die from grief, neglect, abuses, and suffering, at the hands of drunken husbands and fathers, and from diseases inherited from drunken parents, the number of victims will be at least equal to the number of liquor establishments. Every liquor establishment kills one human being; and that one human being loses twenty-two years of the best part of his life.

But counting only one hundred thousand lives, and saying nothing about the time wasted previous to death, there would still be a waste annually of twenty times one hundred thousand, which is two million years of life and industry!

Let those who share in committing or in aiding and abetting this monstrous crime, by their acts, by their words, by their example, or by their silence, tremble in their wickedness.

A grim skeleton is in their houses; the blood of the innocent is upon their hands; and the voice of the murdered right cries out from the tomb against them!

VIII.

ALCOHOL — ITS RESULTS REDUCED TO DOLLARS AND CENTS. — WHAT IS THE VALUE OF THE TIME AND INDUSTRY LOST? — HOW MUCH MONEY DOES IT TAKE TO MAINTAIN HOSPITALS FOR DRUNKEN VAGABONDS? — WHAT IS THE COST OF ASYLUMS FOR LUNATICS AND IDIOTS? — WHAT IS THE COST OF CRIMES AND PRISONS? — HOW MUCH DO WE PAY OUR PAUPERS? — WHAT IS THE VALUE OF THE PROPERTY WE BURN AND DESTROY? — WHO PAYS THE TAXES? — DOES THIS ACCORD WITH JUSTICE, LIBERTY, AND LAW?

VIII.

In this lecture, let us further consider the stupendous facts, as they are set forth in the last one. Let us rearrange and combine these facts, so as to ascertain, more fully, their effects upon the people of the republic.

What effect has alcohol upon the productive industry of the country?

We have already learned that there is a class of three hundred and thirty thousand men who are directly engaged in making and selling liquors, as follows: —

Making distilled liquors,	15,000	men.
Making brewed "	. 15,000	"
Making wines, . .	. 10,000	"
Making foreign .	. 10,000	"

In wholesale trade,	30,000 men.
In retail trade,	250,000 "
Total,	330,000

In one year, therefore, there is the enormous sum of three hundred and thirty thousand years of adult industry thrown into this channel.

The distillers, brewers, and wholesale dealers, numbering fifty thousand men, make their fortunes out of the business, and fifty thousand of the retailers do the same. Adding them together, we have one hundred thousand men who make princely fortunes out of the business. All the rest make barely a comfortable living out of it, and could do just as well or better in some other business.

It takes about ten years, on an average, to make a fortune in the liquor business.

Now since liquors, as shown in Lectures 3, 4, 5, and 6, are so terribly destructive to human health, as to destroy, annually, one hundred thousand lives, as demonstrated in Lecture No. 7, and since those who fall victims to drunkenness die twenty years before their time, it follows that every time one hundred thousand fortunes are made, twenmillion years of human life are wasted; which is equal to sacrificing two hundred years of human life and industry, in order that one man shall amass a fortune!

And this does not take into account the physical and mental diseases, wreck of fortune, and disgrace of family, previous to death. Ten men, each become diseased, debauched, and degraded, and finally die twenty years too soon, in order that one man in the traffic shall amass a fortune. Has justice departed from the earth? Or has the "prince of the powers of darkness" so beclouded the minds of men, that they cannot see where justice is? Are the people in the time of Andrew Johnson superior to the people in the time of Julius Cæsar? How much?

Besides this large sum of direct industry thus engaged, there is a vast amount of industry indirectly engaged in the business. For convenience, let us divide this indirect industry into two divisions, and call it the second and third classes of industry in the liquor trade.

The men composing the second class are engaged in preparing materials with which to build distilleries, breweries, vaults, and cellars, and building the same, including those engaged in making machinery, barrels, and bottles, and in carting and shipping liquors and materials. This second class numbers, perhaps, three hundred and fifty thousand men.

And the third class is engaged in raising sugars, grains, fruits, vegetables, and hops, and in buying and shipping the same to market. These number, perhaps, about three hundred and twenty thousand men. And these three classes, added together, foot up as follows:—

Making and selling liquors,	330,000 men.
Making buildings and machinery,	350,000 "
Raising grains and shipping,	320,000 "
Total,	1,000,000 "

This shows that one million years of industry are annually thus directed. And it shows us that one million people take this means of making a living for themselves.

If the whole business were to be forbidden by law, the first class named above would be thrown out of employment. But it does not follow that they would be seriously injured thereby. Men often quit one business and go into another, and are more prosperous in the second than they were in the first. They would only have to change the direction of their industry. And many of their buildings and much of their machinery could be used in the new direction.

The second class could go on just as they are, piling up buildings and making machinery to fill them; but the buildings and machinery would be for flouring-mills and saw-mills, and for manufacturing other things, such as cotton, woollen, leather, and other goods; and part of the machinery and implements made by this class would be for cars and steamers.

The effect would be to make flour, and lumber, and cotton goods, and woollen goods, and boots and shoes, more abundant, and therefore cheaper; and additional machinery for shipping and travelling being more abundant, shipping and travelling would be less expensive. This, I think, would be the result of turning the productions of the industry of three hundred and fifty thousand mechanics and laborers into other lines of useful industry.

But if flour and lumber are made cheaper, and cotton, woollen, and leather goods are reduced in price, and the means of travelling are made cheaper, who has been injured by the change? Let the defenders of alcohol come before the people and answer, if they dare.

Again; if the grains and fruits raised by three hundred and twenty thousand people, — amounting to sixty-two million bushels, as shown in Lecture No. 7, — if all these are not fermented (rotted) and distilled, they will remain in the market as provisions and feed. People will raise more stock and feed them better with part of the surplus grain, which will increase the quantity of meat, and of course reduce the price; the remainder of the extra fruits and grains will remain upon the market as provisions for men; and the quantity being increased, the price will be reduced in proportion.

Well, if meat becomes cheaper, and bread becomes cheaper, and fruits become cheaper, and all kinds of clothing cheaper, and tools, conveniences, and comforts are all multiplied and reduced in price, "who is hurt" by the operation? Tell me, — who is abused?

Wheat is now worth two dollars a bushel, and a good cook-stove is worth forty dollars, so that twenty bushels of wheat will buy a cook-stove. Now, supposing we stop the distilleries and breweries, and the price of wheat comes down to one dollar a bushel, and we put the distillers and their steam-machinery to making stoves, until they are reduced to twenty dollars. Who is hurt? Twenty bushels of wheat will still buy a cook-stove, the same as before. There is more wheat in the world, and more stoves to cook it in. So that many people who could before hardly afford to buy either wheat or stove, will now be able to have both. Please tell me, who is damaged?

Men who have families can provide for them more easily; and there will be some inducement for young men and bachelors to marry. Will that hurt anybody?

What do you work for, anyhow? What do you live for? If you have plenty to eat, good clothes to wear, comfortable shelter, a good healthy place to sleep, and are surrounded by fat horses and cattle, and supplied with all kinds of comforts, conveniences, and luxuries, what more do you want?

Some people are so shamefully ignorant, and so contemptibly mean, that if they owned a square mile of heaven, with all its joys, they would not be satisfied until they had swapped it for a small vacant lot on one of the back alleys of hell. I do not wish to flatter such people or I would call them stupid.

Only one hundred thousand men make fortunes out of the business, while thirty-one million nine hundred thousand lose by the traffic, as they have to pay more for the necessaries and comforts of life than they would if it were suppressed. Thus we see that three hundred and twenty men lose, in order that one man may make. Is that fair? Is that economy?

But supposing that all who are engaged in the liquor traffic, directly and indirectly, made more money than they could in any other way, to the full number of one million men, while all the rest of the people were losers, is *that* fair? Is it right to tax thirty-one people, in order to enrich one person, and that one no better than the rest? Would it be fair to tax four persons to enrich us? What becomes of the good old democratic maxim, "The greatest good of the greatest number"?

Is it fair, even, to tax *one* man to enrich another? If so, then what, in the name of all that is holy, do you understand by the words justice and equity?

But let us take another view of the subject. Let us open the books and examine the accounts. What is the cost of our alcoholic liquors in cash?

LOSS OF INDUSTRY.

Suppose that a day's labor is worth one dollar and board, and that there are three hundred working days in a year. Then the one million people engaged in the liquor business would be worth three hundred million dollars a year. And the two million years of life and health (and therefore industry) that are annually destroyed, would be worth six hundred million dollars, or a total of nine hundred million dollars.

COST OF INSANITY.

The building of asylums, and furnishing medicines and comforts for four thousand insane people, who die after three years of insanity, at an average cost of one thousand dollars a year for each lunatic, amounts to twelve million dollars a year. And at the same rate for the eight thousand lunatics who do not die, but who are cured after three years of treatment in the asylum, twenty-four million dollars. Making a total of thirty-six million dollars, as the annual cost of the insanity caused by drunkenness.

COST OF IDIOCY.

Add to this the cost of feeding, clothing, and providing for twelve thousand idiots or fools, at an average cost of five hundred dollars a year for each fool, six million dollars. But if these fools had been rational beings, we should have had their industry, worth three hundred dollars each a year. Suppose the average age of a fool to be thirty years (a shortening of life not heretofore considered), it follows that during the last ten years of his life — from the age of twenty to thirty — he could have earned three thousand dollars. And the whole number of fools, at this rate, could have earned thirty-six million dollars. All this is lost industry. Adding the cost of maintaining them, and the loss of their ten years' industry (and it should be more than ten), we have forty-two million dollars, as the annual cost of the idiocy of drunkenness.

COST OF CRIME.

The expense of arresting, confining, convicting, and executing four hundred murderers every year, at an average cost of five thousand dollars each, amounts to two million dollars. The expense of building — more especially of enlarging — and guarding forty State prisons, and detecting, arresting, convicting, and maintaining the twenty thousand convicts confined therein, for crimes committed through the agency of liquors, at an average cost of seven hundred dollars a year for each convict, amounts to fourteen million dollars. The expense of enlarging jails, and detecting, arresting, feeding, trying, and punishing persons for two hundred thousand minor crimes and misdemeanors, committed through intoxication, at an average of one hundred dollars each, amounts to twenty million dollars. Making a total annual cost of the crimes of intoxication, about thirty-six million dollars.

COST OF PUBLIC HOSPITALS.

Let us add the cost of building and supporting two hundred hospitals for one hundred thousand people, who ruin their health and squander their fortunes for drink, and corrupt themselves with filthy diseases, which have to be cured or the patient buried at public expense, at the rate of one hundred dollars for each patient, amounts to ten million dollars annually.

COST OF PAUPERISM.

We must not fail to take into account the cost of maintaining five hundred thousand paupers, who become paupers through the agency of drunkenness. Part of those are supported by direct taxation, and part by public and private charity, and at the rate of one hundred dollars a year for each pauper, amounts to fifty million dollars annually.

LOSSES BY ACCIDENTS.

Nor must we fail to take into consideration the vast amount of property, in buildings, vessels, goods, and provisions, that are burned, sunk, and destroyed every year, through the drunkenness of owners and agents (and many lives are lost in this way, not heretofore considered), the loss of which property often falls heavily upon innocent parties, who never use liquors themselves, and therefore is in the nature of a tax upon sober people, amounting to over fifty million dollars more.

Now, let us add up these various items of cost, and see what the whole amount will look like:—

Loss of time and industry,	$900,000,000
Cost of insanity,	36,000,000
Cost of idiocy,	42,000,000
Cost of crime,	36,000,000
Cost of sickness in hospitals,	10,000,000
Cost of pauperism,	50,000,000
Losses by accidents,	50,000,000
Total cost of drunkenness,	$1,124,000,000

Call it an even billion. A billion a year! And those who have followed me through these lectures will not say this is an over-estimate.

And all this in order to gratify a perverted appetite for a noxious article, and to allow one hundred thousand men to accumulate vast fortunes.

If we should leave off (though why should we?) the first item in the above sum, we still have to pay, annually, over two hundred millions of dollars, which is a tax upon honest and temperate people?

You all know that during the year 1867 the liquor men did not pay but one-twentieth of their share even, of these enormous taxes, either local or national.

Is that justice? Is it right that you should be forced to pay such heavy taxes, to support a God-condemned and hell-deserving incubus upon society, that you hate and abhor, and that injures two hundred and ninety-nine people where it benefits but one? Is that justice?

Are you a free people, and submit to such outrages? He who knowingly submits to a monstrous and infamous injustice, without protest, is either a slave, or a coward, or both combined.

What becomes of your boasted liberty, if you have to bow, and cringe, and pay forcible tribute to a hateful and cruel despotism?

What is liberty? I understand liberty to be the right to do as you please, so far as you can without interfering with other people's equal right to do as they please; the right to do as you desire, provided you do not injure others; the right to do whatever is right.

Now, if the whole entire liquor traffic were prohibited by law, we should not only have two hundred thousand dollars less local taxes and losses to pay, but we should have better health, sounder morals, longer life, and two hundred thousand dollars more to pay with,—making a vast difference in our favor.

Is it right for one set of men to interfere with the rights of another set in this way?

What is law? Blackstone says, "Law is a rule of action, emanating from the supreme power of the State, commanding what is right and prohibiting what is wrong." Liberty says, you may do whatever is right. Law says, you shall do whatever is right. The one permits and the other commands the practice of the great principle of right. You may and shall do right; but you may not, and shall not do wrong. So say liberty and law. But the liquor business comes forward and says, like this:—

"Hear, all ye people of the world!

Hear! I claim the right to load the bodies of men with a slow, lingering disease, so that after ten years of suffering, they shall die some horrible and disgraceful death, at the rate of one hundred thousand a year; I claim the right to injure the minds of men, so as to send twelve thousand raving maniacs to the lunatic asylum, and twelve thousand more to the asylum for idiots; I claim the right to so madden the people with ungovernable frenzy, as to make six hundred kill themselves; but before they die, to kill, with heartless ferocity, four hundred innocent victims, and make six hundred more perish with fierce and wild delirium; I claim the right, during the ten years these people are drinking themselves to death, to send one hundred thousand of them to the hospitals with disease, to make them squander their money and property, and the money and property of their families, and waste their time and shorten their lives, amounting to three million years of life and industry; I claim the right, during the same ten years, to cause the people to commit a vast number of heinous crimes and offences, so as to keep twenty thousand in the state prisons of the land, and to cause two hundred thousand petty crimes and misdemeanors against the peace and good order of society, and make them harsh and cruel to their once-loved wives and helpless babes; I claim the right to make five hundred thousand paupers and beggars, so as to crush out their dignity and self-respect, and blight their hopes forever; I claim the right to destroy with midnight flames, vast amounts of property by land and sea; I claim the right to tax the honest and temperate people of the country, without their consent, to pay for all these woes and calamities, to the amount of two hundred million dollars a year; I claim the right to refuse to pay more than one-twentieth of the taxes which the laws of the land have assessed as my share, and the right to force honest people to pay them for me; I claim to be above the law and beyond the law; I claim the right to dwarf the intellect and corrupt the morals of the people, and corrupt the hearts of the lawgivers, and corrupt those whom the people elect to enforce the laws; and I not only claim these rights, but, in the name of wickedness, my birthright, and depravity, my acquired knowledge, and passion, my strength, and covetousness, the grand aim of my life, I will exercise these rights, law or no law; for I have usurped the authority to rule and ruin the earth! Hear, people, hear!"

IX.

Alcohol — Is it ever adulterated or counterfeited? — What are some of the Substances used in its Adulteration? — Are any of these Substances Poison? — What are organic vegetable Alkalies? — Are they cheaper than Alcohol itself? — How much cheaper? — To what Extent are alcoholic Liquors adulterated? — Is it a Crime to put deadly Poisons in Liquors?

IX.

LET us now pursue our subject — alcohol — into another field; the field where it becomes counterfeited and adulterated with other substances, more deadly than itself.

On passing the outer gates of this field, we notice that it is a rough and forbidding region, traversed by deep and dark ravines, out of which lead broad caves and gloomy caverns, in which are scattered a wilderness of bones.

Our visit into this broken wilderness is no pleasure trip, no holiday journey for the gratification of romantic ideas, into the wild regions of nature; but rather a deliberate, though reluctant invasion of the jungles and caverns and fortifications of a deadly foe.

Without an invitation, we propose to enter the dragon-guarded labyrinths, where the infernal monster hides. Hitherto we have considered our subject in the light of a regular business, the same as any other article of trade and commerce. We now come to examine that part of it where deliberate, premeditated fraud is committed, in making drugged, counterfeited, and adulterated shams, down in dingy rooms, where the doors are barred and guarded, where the conversation is in whispers, and where winks, nods, and secrecy, cover up a deep-dyed and deliberate villany, compared with which, all that has been said against alcohol, in the foregoing lectures, becomes commonplace and tame.

Open and high-handed rascality may be considered honorable, when compared with that which goes down, deliberately, into concealed cellars, and in darkness develops its infernal schemes for accomplishing wickedness and crime.

If a man counterfeits a dollar-bill, you arrest him, try him, and send him to the penitentiary. And yet he has only defrauded a few people out of their property or money, by giving, in exchange, the worthless bills.

No person's health is injured, no one's mind is deranged, nobody's days are shortened, no life is taken, but only a little property lost by this false and sham equivalent, — that is all.

But you punish the man who counterfeits money, by close confinement and hard labor in prison; and you confiscate and destroy his dies and plates, and burn all his false paper, by order of the courts of law.

Then why not arrest and punish the man, — I beg pardon; I do not wish to disgrace the name of "man" in that way, — why not punish the vile miscreant who counterfeits intoxicating liquors?

He counterfeits an article that is to be taken into the human stomach; that is to pass into the human heart; that is to be filtered through the human liver; that is to circulate in the human blood. He puts poisonous drugs into his counterfeits, that injure human health, and shorten human life.

Why do you not punish *him?* Why should one counterfeiter be arrested and punished, while a worse one is permitted to follow his infamous trade?

In many of our cities it is the law that if a market-woman adulterates her butter, by putting lard in the middle of the lump, she shall be arrested, have her adulterated mixture confiscated, and be fined for fraud. How ready those cities are to punish a poor woman for a little, petty adulteration of an article of food, although she merely mixes another article of food!

Suppose she were to mix in a little strychnine, — what a monstrous hue-and-cry there would be raised! The pictorial papers would have her likeness engraved, and emblazon it as "The Great Female Demon!"

What has she done? "She has put lard in her butter, and mixed in a little strychnine, and sold it, — the hussy; and *made two cents clear*, by the nefarious operation!"

But the business of adulterating intoxicating liquors is largely carried on, in almost every city and village in the republic, into which strychnine and other poisons are mixed, causing extensive injuries to the health of the people, and destroying many lives, in order that the counterfeiters may accumulate vast wealth by wickedness and fraud.

Why not pounce upon these, with the same ferocity that you would upon the poor butter-woman? Are you afraid of the scoundrels? Or do you not know how to detect them? Is it cowardice? Or is it ignorance? Or has the morality of this people become so stultified, that they wilfully sustain partiality, injustice, and wrong? Consistency is a jewel. Let us try to possess it.

Why do people adulterate liquors? Why? To obtain money without returning an equivalent, of course, the same as in all other varieties of fraud.

And therefore the articles used must be cheaper than the liquors themselves.

And what are these articles? What are liquors adulterated with?

To answer this question we must subdivide it. There is one set of ingredients, used to adulterate the alcohol itself;

another set used to give the color; and others to give age and bead; and all to deceive.

If you wanted to convert one gallon of new corn whiskey into four gallons of old peach brandy, you would use one set of ingredients; into old Jamaica rum, another set; into best Holland gin, another set; and if you wanted to convert it into ten gallons of old port wine, you would use still another set of ingredients, though the one used in the place of alcohol might be the same in all cases. The coloring and flavoring would be different, though the "drunk" ingredient might be the same. These ingredients, and the receipts for using them, are extensively known among liquor men, and just as extensively used.

And first, as to the adulterating of alcohol itself,—"the thing what makes the drunk come."

We have shown, in Lectures No. 1 and 2, that alcohol is an irritant or stimulating poison, vegetable in its origin, and narcotic in its tendency.

It follows naturally that any other poison that is irritant or stimulating in its action, vegetable in its origin, and narcotic in its tendency, will produce similar, if not identical effects.

They must irritate the membranes of the body, benumb sensation, and make one dizzy; and in larger doses must interfere with motion.

There are a number of poisons that will answer the description, and do all these things. They are generally called, in the dispensatories and chemistries, the "organic vegetable alkalies," but are sometimes called poisons, sometimes called vegetable irritants, sometimes called narcotics, sometimes called stimulant narcotics, sometimes called anodyne narcotics, and some of them are called by other names. The following are prominent among them :—

   STRYCHNINE,
   STRAMONIUM,
   BELLADONNA,
   TOBACCO,
   COCCULUS,
   OPIUM.

Now, as the action of all these organic vegetable alkalies upon the human system, is very similar to alcohol, it follows that when combined with alcohol, so as to increase the quantity, by taking the place of that article, the effect will be about the same.

Let us notice one fact. A bushel of the sweetest and best corn will only make three gallons of pure whiskey.

But since the distillers have learned how

to mix strychnine in their yeast, with which they ferment their "mash" (corn meal and warm water), they have been able to average four gallons to the bushel; which is now the average throughout the land.

This shows that twenty-five per cent. of what purports to be the alcoholic strength of the common corn whiskey of the country is, in reality, its strychnine strength!

Strychnine is so very strong that it takes but little of it, when added to the bushel of corn, to make the additional gallon of whiskey. Three cents' worth of strychnine and a gallon of water, added to the original three gallons of whiskey from a bushel, makes four gallons from a bushel; and all sold to the people for pure whiskey!

Is that fraud? Or what would you call it? Is it a legitimate transaction? Call it what you will, there stands the naked fact.

One drug-house in London, last year, sold to one liquor firm in that city more strychnine than the whole medical profession of the city would require in the same time.

You all remember, only a few years ago, when the distillers in the Miami Valley undertook to make five or six and even seven gallons of whiskey out of a bushel of corn, by adding more strychnine; and as some of the additional strychnine remained in the slop, it killed the hogs.

They overdid the thing a little,—that was all.

Vast quantities of strychnine are still used in most of the distilleries of the country; but the hogs get less of it, and do not often die.

But the man who drinks four gallons of corn whiskey now, drinks one gallon of strychnine and water.

No wonder pork is unhealthy. No wonder drunkards die. No wonder distillers get rich.

Strychnine is found in a number of substances, but chiefly in the seeds and bark of the nux vomica tree, and the bean of Saint Ignatius. These plants are now extensively cultivated, and their product enters largely into the trade of the druggists. For further particulars with regard to it, and its effects upon the human system, I refer you to the United States Dispensatory, and the American Dispensatory, found in all drug stores, and also to the various medical dictionaries and materia medicas in your family physician's library.

Talk about "pure whiskey, right fresh from the distillery!" People who talk thus do not know what they are talking about. There is very little — if any — "pure whiskey" made.

ITS NATURE AND EFFECTS. 343

Stramonium is, perhaps, the next most popular poison in adulterating liquors. This is made from the juice of a poisonous weed, which grows almost everywhere, and is therefore cheap. It is sometimes called Jimson weed, and sometimes thorn-apple weed, and grows of its own accord by the roadside, and in vacant lots everywhere. It is kept in the drug-stores in the form of fluid, or solid extract of stramonium.

This poison, although extensively used in the yeast of the distilleries the same as strychnine, is far more generally used in the retail shops. Receipts for making stramonium whiskey are sold by fourth-rate chemists to the retailers at enormous prices.

A retailer buys a gallon of corn whiskey, the intoxicating strength of which is already one-fourth strychnine, and proceeds, according to receipt, to make two gallons out of it, by adding stramonium and water!

But as stramonium is likely to cramp the stomach of the drinker, a little opium is added to prevent cramping, and a little potash has to be added to counteract the peculiar taste and smell, — the ingredients costing four or five cents.

Some folks think this is an honest business; and some folks don't. Just owing to how you were raised and educated.

Two fishermen, in a little town on the Ohio River, bought a pint of whiskey and went up the river to fish. That afternoon they were both found, on the bank of the river, dead. The bottle was empty. When the retailer heard they were dead, he immediately emptied that keg of whiskey into a ditch. As the proof was destroyed, of course he was not found guilty. In all probability he, through mistake, put more stramonium into the strychnine whiskey than he intended, or perhaps forgot to add the requisite amount of water. The fishermen are dead, and who is to blame?

As some of you will not take the trouble to examine the United States Dispensatory for yourselves, I will read a few passages from that standard work: —

"Stramonium is a powerful narcotic. When taken in quantities sufficient to affect the system moderately, it usually produces more or less cerebral disturbance, indicated by vertigo (dizziness, or swimming of the head), headache, dimness or perversion of vision, and confusion of thought, sometimes amounting to a slight delirium, or a species of intoxication. A disposition to sleep is sometimes, but not uniformly, produced. When taken in poisonous doses, this narcotic produces cardialgia, excessive thirst, nausea and vomiting; a sense of strangulation, anxiety, and faintness; partial or complete blindness, with dilatation of the pupil; vertigo, delirium, sometimes of a furious, sometimes of a whimsical character, tremors of the limbs, palsy, and ultimately stupor and convulsions. From all these symptoms the patient may recover; but in numerous instances they have terminated in death. It has long been known as a poisonous and intoxicating herb."

There it is in plain English: "A poisonous and intoxicating herb."

Is that new to you? Those same words have been printed and lying on the counters of all your drug-stores for more than forty years. And it has been known to the knowing ones in the liquor business for twice forty years. And they have been making good use of their knowledge, as shown in the fact that they have amassed vast fortunes, while your sons and brothers have gone to early graves.

Can you respect and love a man who makes and sells to your young and inexperienced son a mixture of alcohol, strychnine, stramonium, opium, and water, which makes him sick and delirious, or perhaps takes his young life? Your organ of friendship is stronger than mine, if you can.

Belladonna sometimes goes by the name of deadly nightshade. It is a perennial plant, and grows everywhere, — in shady places, in the fence-corners, and by the side of walls. Its berry, when ripe, is a dark-purple, and has a sweetish taste. The whole thing is poison, — roots, stalks, leaves, berries and all. Let me read a little from the United States Dispensatory: —

"The action of belladonna is that of a powerful narcotic. It has little intensity of local action, but is absorbed; and, entering the circulation, exercises its influence upon the nervous system, especially upon the brain. Among its first obvious effects, when taken in the usual dose, and continued for some time, are dryness and stricture of the fauces and neighboring parts, with slight uneasiness or giddiness of the head, and more or less dimness of vision. In large quantities, belladonna is capable of producing the most deleterious effects. It is, in fact, a powerful poison, and many instances are recorded in which it has been accidentally swallowed, or purposely administered, with fatal consequences. Soon after the poison has been swallowed, its peculiar influence is experienced, in dryness of the mouth and fauces, great thirst, difficult deglutition, nausea, and ineffectual retching, vertigo, intoxication, or delirium, attended with violent gestures, and sometimes with fits of laughter, and followed with a comatose (benumbed and sleepy or stupid and drowsy) state."

There you have it, in good old English: "Intoxication or delirium, attended with violent gestures, and sometimes with loud laughter, and followed with drowsiness, stupidity, and insensibility."

Did you ever see any one act in that way after drinking the common liquors of your market? You all have.

Most drinkers, when they go into a saloon, expect to get something "that will make the drunk come." And they are not particular what it is. The shrewd men in the liquor business have known, for the last fifty years, that belladonna would "fetch the drunk," and have arranged their business accordingly.

Now, as belladonna grows wild everywhere, and can be easily obtained, and as it is so powerful that just a little bit of it will make a gallon of drunk-water, it follows that it must be cheap.

About two cents' worth will make a gallon of liquor, which sells in our market, at wholesale, for a dollar and a half.

You will find it in the drug-stores in the shape of fluid and solid extract of belladonna.

A distiller sells a gallon of strychnine whiskey to a wholesaler. While in the wholesaler's warehouse it is made into two gallons of whiskey, by adding stramonium and opium, the additional gallon costing three or four cents. Then it is sold to the retailer. In the retailer's back cellar it is again adulterated and made into four gallons, by adding belladonna, the two additional gallons costing two or three cents each.

Retailed at ten cents a drink, the profits are tolerably handsome, I thank you!

Only about six or seven dollars' profit on each gallon.

Perhaps you call that a legitimate transaction. Well, some people will have queer notions. I was not brought up in that way. My early education must have been sadly neglected.

You will arrest a market-woman for putting four ounces of lard into a pound of butter, — will you? But strychnine whiskey, adulterated with stramonium, and belladonna, and opium, is legitimate. Shame, shame!

The Legislature of Ohio directed Dr. Hiram Cox, a distinguished chemist of Cincinnati, to analyze and examine the liquors in that market. He labored more than two years; but, meanwhile, the liquor men brought their influence to bear upon the legislature so as to suppress his report, and it has never been published. But he has written a number of letters, from one of which, written to James Black, of Lancaster, Penn., I will read a few lines :—

"I was appointed to the office of Chemical Inspector on the 19th of March, 1855. Since then I have made over six hundred inspections of stores, and lots of liquors, of every variety, and now positively assert that over ninety per cent. of all that I have analyzed were adulterated with the most pernicious and poisonous ingredients!"

I shall not have time to quote very much from him, but will only take time to quote one out of the host of his experiments. He says, "I called at a grocery store one day, where liquor was being sold. A couple of Irishmen came in while I was there, and called for some whiskey. The first one drank, and the moment he drank, the tears flowed freely, while he, at the same time, caught his breath like one suffocating or strangling. When he could speak, he said to his companion, 'Och, Michael, by the powers but this is warming to the stoomach, sure!' Michael drank, and went through like contortions, with the remark, 'Troth, and wouldn't it be foin on a could frosty morning, Timothy?' After they had drank I asked the proprietor to pour me out a little in a tumbler. I went to my office, got my instruments, and examined it. I found it seventeen per cent. alcoholic spirits, when it should have been fifty, and the difference in percentage was made up by sulphuric acid, red pepper, pelitory, caustic potash, brucine, and one of the salts of nux vomica (strychnine). One pint of such liquor (at one time) would kill the strongest man. I had the manufacturer indicted. But by such villany he has become wealthy; and I never have, owing to some defect in the law, been able to bring that case to a final issue."

Cocculus is the fruit of an East Indian plant. It is sometimes called cocculus indicus, and sometimes animesta.

Ten thousand pounds of it were shipped to Great Britain in a single year, and used in adulterating liquors. With that article our British cousins made not less than one hundred and fifty thousand barrels of beer, equal to six million gallons. Mr. Morris, a London brewer, says, "Cocculus is used as a substitute for both malt and hops." Let us read from the United States Dispensatory: "Cocculus acts upon the system in the same manner of the other acrid, narcotic poisons (such as strychnine, stramonium, belladonna, tobacco, opium, and others), but is never given (as a medicine) internally. In India they put it into the water so as to stupefy the fishes, in order that they may be caught. It has been given to dogs, in the quantity of five or ten grains, and produced convulsions and death. In Europe it is said to be added to malt liquors, in order to give them bitterness and intoxicating properties; although the practice is forbidden by law, in England, under heavy penalties."

Thus reads the Dispensatory. But perhaps you were not aware of the fact that it is, at this hour, extensively used, not only in England, and throughout all Europe, but largely in the United States, for adulterating all kinds of intoxicating liquors. And it would be still more largely used here if it were cheaper. The depravity of the depraved is cunning and ingenious in searching out the means for accomplishing fraud.

We now come to tobacco, which is cheaper yet, and easier to get hold of. Perhaps you were not aware that immense quantities of liquors were adulterated with "dog-leg." Well, such is the unfortunate fact.

One of our regiments at Savannah, Georgia, took possession of a whiskey-shop, where the drunken rebels had been getting their whiskey. Quite a number of our "naughty boys" got on a bender, from the same hogshead of liquor. They found it would make a Union man drunk just the same as it had a rebel. When the liquor was all gone and the cask empty, one of our naughty ones smashed the head in. And what did he find in the bottom? He found about fifteen or twenty pounds of dog-leg tobacco. It was well soaked, having been there perhaps a year or so. There are perhaps five hundred witnesses to this fact.

If I had time, I could furnish you with a number of similar facts. There is a young man, living less than fifty miles from Chicago, who told me that his father owned a large brewery for twelve years, and that he worked in the same all that time. He told me that the largest bills his father had to pay were not for malt, nor for hops, but for tobacco. The young man has quit the business, but still retains the fortune thus acquired.

Cocculus and tobacco are more extensively used in adulterating colored liquors, such as red brandies, red wines, and ale and beer. When used in white liquors, it has to be chemically decomposed, so as to take out the coloring matters, — the same as strychnine.

Tobacco is likely to act as an emetic, if partaken of too freely; and hence it is necessary to neutralize its emetic property by adding a little opium or stramonium.

Do you remember, when you chewed your first chew, or smoked your first cigar, how drunk you got? Some of us do. The liquor men, greedy for money, learned, fifty years ago, that tobacco was one of the things that would " make the drunk come." The weed is so well known that I need scarcely mention its various qualities, but simply state that it is a sedative, narcotic poison, and one of the " organic vegetable alkalies," that so much resemble each other. You will find full descriptions of it in the dispensatories and materia medicas.

Besides these substances, there are many others used, in the adulteration of liquors, as a substitute for alcohol, to the number of twenty-five or thirty. Such, for instance, as digitalis, arnica, coca, aconite, and dracontium; besides a number of minerals and mineral acids. The Dispensatory says, in one place, that " proof-spirits are very far from being pure;" and in another place advises physicians not to use them, in compounding medicines, " on account of their impurities."

What would you think of a currency, nine-tenths of which were counterfeit? Or provisions, nine-tenths of which were diseased or poisoned?

And what would you do with the men who were engaged in counterfeiting money or provisions? You would stop them, would you? Well, then, why do you not stop those who are counterfeiting drinks? Provisions and drinks all go into the same stomach. And poison is just as injurious in the one as the other. Why not govern them both by the same laws?

X

Alcohol — Are there many Articles used in imitating it? — What are Some of them? — To what Extent is Adulteration carried on? — How do you know? — Have you got any responsible Authorities? — Who? — Any Books? — What Books? — Can you detect these Frauds? — How? — What about Chemistry? — Should deliberate Fraud be punished? — What is the Duty of a free People?

X.

FREDERICK ACCUM, the great chemist and lecturer of London, published a book, years ago, on this subject. From his book, on page 185, let me read these words: "To increase the intoxicating quality of beer (and other liquors), the deleterious vegetable substance called cocculus indicus, and the extract of this same poisonous berry, technically called black extract, or by some hard multum, are employed. opium, tobacco, nux vomica (strychnine), and extract of poppies (cheap opium), have also been used."

Well, that helps to confirm what we said in Lecture No. 9.

Besides the organic vegetable alkalies, such as strychnine, stramonium, belladonna, cocculus, tobacco, opium, coca, and others, there are many other articles used in the adulteration of liquors. Their name is legion. Almost every distiller, rectifier, vintner, brewer, warehouseman, and retailer in the whole country, has bought or sold receipts for adulterating. Some of these ingredients are as villanous and as vile as those just now mentioned. Others are comparatively innocent.

I have made out a list of a few of the leading articles, and prominent among them stands fusil oil, which is largely used, in connection with the organic vegetable alkalies, to make what is called "rot gut," or "forty-rod" whiskey, — and well named.

INGREDIENTS OF A WARMING NATURE.

Pepper, capsicum, cloves, ginger, spice, vinegar, acetic acid, tartaric acid, citric acid, butyric acid, cream of tartar, nitric acid or aqua-fortis, sulphuric acid, prussic acid, sulphuric ether, nitric ether, acetic ether, spirits of nitre, oil of vitriol, oil of turpentine, oil of cassia, oil of caraway, oil of cloves, extract of japonica, extract of bitter almonds, extract of orris root, extract of angelican root, grains of paradise, multum, poppy seeds, juniper berries, aloes, cochineal, black ants, and Spanish juice.

TO GIVE TASTE AND ASTRINGENCY.

Bruised raisins, dried blackberries, dried peaches, dried cherries, orange-peel, coriander seed, white oak bark, tannic acid, kino, rhatany, catechu, caraway seed, cardamom seed, fennel seed, wormwood, alum, copperas, sulphate of iron, and sulphate of copper.

TO CORRECT UNNATURAL TASTES.

Lime-water, carbonate of lime, carbonate of soda, nitrate of potash, caustic potash, pearlash, saleratus, sugar of lead, and litharge.

COLORING MATTERS.

Burnt sugar, beet-juice, dried apples, dried peaches, elderberries, treacle, red saunders, logwood, and sulphuric acid.

That is perhaps enough, though by no means all, of the ingredients used in these adulterations.

It is a very common thing to adulterate, or imitate one liquor by mixing in another — cheaper one.

We have already shown, in Lectures No. 1 and 2, that wine, or liquor of any kind, will not be certain to keep, if exposed to transportation, unless it has at least twenty per cent. alcoholic strength.

But the "pure fermented juice of the grape" never has that much in it by nature. Therefore whiskey or brandy is poured into it until it does have that amount of alcoholic strength, so as to enable it to bear exposure and travel. Hence we see that all the wines in the market must first be strengthened or adulterated by mixing them with stronger liquors. Any one, who thinks at all, can see from this that there is very little, if any, "pure wine" in the market.

True, it does not necessarily follow that it is all adulterated with the sham decoctions described in Lecture No. 9; but whether it "necessarily follows," or not, we shall soon see whether such is the fact.

Besides the fact that nearly all the wines

in the market are strengthened with brandy or whiskey, so as to make them keep, there is another series of facts tending to prove extensive adulterations; namely, that there is perhaps nearly a hundred times as much "port wine" sold and drank as can be made from all the grapes raised in the region of Oporto, including the whole Douro Valley. The wine merchants of Oporto buy other inferior wines and adulterate their own with them, adding beet whiskey, potato whiskey, fig whiskey, and water, sweetening the same with sugar of lead or litharge, and coloring the same with burnt sugar, elderberries, treacle, logwood, and the tincture of red saunders. In this way the wine manufacturers and merchants of Oporto manage to ship about five times as much as grows in the whole Douro Valley "Port wine" with a vengeance!

In proof of this I refer you to the lec

tures of Rev. Eliphalet Nott, former President of Union College, at Schenectady, New York, where a mass of facts and figures on the subject are presented. Also to a book entitled, "Tricks of the Trade," published by Routlidge, Wason, and Routlidge, on Farringdon Street, London, and 56 Walker Street, New York, in which a still larger mass of testimony is presented, showing the wholesale and villanous adulterations of "port wine" in the very city and valley where it is made. Port wine, indeed!

Another fact. The city of London, in 1866, with her two and a half millions of people, drank twice as much "port wine" as was shipped from the whole Douro Valley in the same year, counting the good and bad and all together. This shows that the famous wines of Oporto, already increased by adulterations to five times their bulk, were doubled in quantity again, in the city of London alone. How are you, port wine?

During the same year, the city of New York, with her million people, drank and sold about the same quantity that was made and adulterated in the whole Douro Valley!

So that we have already accounted for three times the quantity shipped from Portugal, and have only considered the markets of London and New York. And as the quantity originally shipped was five times too great, it follows that we have accounted for three times five, which is fifteen times as much "port wine" as can be made from all the grapes of the Douro. And yet we have considered only two of the great wine markets of the world.

Strange that an intelligent people will let themselves be gulled in this way. If the Douro River were a thousand miles long, instead of only sixty miles, it could not furnish grapes enough to make all this ocean of "port wine." The whole world of fashionable topers, and invalids, and imbeciles, are drinking wine made out of the little handful of grapes grown on the banks of a small creek in Portugal!

The miracle of feeding five thousand souls from "five loaves and three small fishes," and having plenty left, is a small, cheap, commonplace transaction. The expansion of "port wine" beats the "loaves and fishes!"

The United States Dispensatory says: "Considerable quantities of brandy are usually added to port wine, which causes its heating quality on the palate. It is sometimes made of a small proportion of real port wine, mixed with cider, juice of elderberries, and brandy, and colored and rendered astringent with logwood and alum."

That from the Dispensatory! And other medical and chemical authors tell us that "all kinds of wine are largely adulterated; and sugar of lead is extensively used to sweeten the adulterations."

Well, now, imagine a gallon of real, genuine port wine is taken from the wine-press on the banks of the Douro, to a warehouse in Oporto. There it is made into five gallons by adding beet whiskey, elderberry juice, and water; it is then shipped to a London Dock warehouse, where it is made into ten gallons by adding potato whiskey, cocculus, and water, and colored with treacle and red saunders; thence it goes to a New York warehouse, where it is made into twenty gallons by adding strychnine, or belladonna, whiskey, and opium, and colored with logwood. Then it comes to a wholesale warehouse in Chicago, where it is made into forty gallons, by adding more strychnine, stramonium, belladonna, whiskey, and water, and colored with red saunders, logwood, and sulphuric acid. Then it goes to a retail shop on Clark Street, where it is made into eighty gallons, by adding tobacco-juice, burnt sugar, alum, and sugar of lead.

It now has, as the Dispensatory truly says, "a very little pure wine" in it, but is only a heterogeneous mass of third-rate chemicals.

At this point a Wabash Avenue deacon buys a part of it for sacramental purposes, and takes it to the sanctuary; and you and I are invited to partake of this delicious and delightful nectar, in order to commemorate the purity and holiness of One who "came to redeem the world from sin," and who said to the wayward people of the world, "All things whatsoever ye would that men should do unto you, do ye even so unto them."

What becomes of the beautiful words of Jesus, at the last supper, when giving the cup to his disciples he said, "I will not drink henceforth of this fruit of the vine, until that day when I shall drink it new with you, in my Father's kingdom"? Beautiful, beautiful! "I will not drink henceforth this *fruit of the vine!*" Well, is this heterogeneous conglomerate of poisons, drugs, and dye-stuffs, the "fruit of the vine"? God help the vine that bears such fruit as that! "Until that day when I shall drink it *new* with you, in my Father's kingdom." N-e-w, new! What does the word NEW mean in that passage? If it means anything, it means *new* "fruit of the vine!" — fresh, new juice of the grape! — unfermented wine, just as it comes from the grape!

How easy to squeeze new, sweet juice out of ripe grapes, heat it hot and can it up, so as to have it pure, sweet, and new, for the communion table!

Such a sacrament as that I trust I shall always be worthy to take along with those who hope to be rewarded, according to their deeds, in the realm of departed spirits beyond the grave; but fermented, adulterated, poisoned, and counterfeited slop I never will take at the communion table again, so help me, God! The minister of the gospel, who, through ignorance, gives such loathsome, counterfeit trash to his flock, and calls it the "fruit of the vine," and thinks it is new, deserves the pity of all intelligent people, and should be forgiven; but the clergyman who gives it knowingly, is neither a Christian nor an honest man, but a base hypocrite, so treacherous to the principles of truth and righteousness as to deserve the contempt of all good and faithful citizens.

So much for "port wine." And what we have said of this is almost equally true of most other wines. Talk about Madeira wine! The whole island of Madeira only ships about twenty-five thousand barrels a year, and less than one-fifth of this is "pure" when it leaves the island. All the rest is counterfeited and adulterated, about the same as port wine, before it goes on board the vessel. And if God ever pities anything that is abused, he certainly pities poor Madeira wine, after it passes through three or four wholesale establishments, and has been three days in a retailer's cellar!

One gallon has changed into a hundred; and it would take an industrious and first-class chemist at least a week to detect and describe the poisons and adulterations; taste, flavor, bouquet, bead, age, intoxicating qualities, — all counterfeit.

And the same of sherry, Champagne, claret, and Burgundy, — the whole brood.

Did you know there is nearly as much California wine in St. Louis and Chicago, as there is pressed in all California? Not one gallon in a hundred ever saw California. Not one gallon in a hundred ever heard of a grape.

A druggist in Cincinnati, Ohio, sent to New York for two hogsheads of seignette brandy, so as to supply the physicians with the very best article for medical purposes. One cask was dark seignette, the other pale seignette. Dr. Cox, the chemist, tested them; poured some into a tumbler; sunk a polished steel blade into it, and let it remain there fifteen minutes. At the end of that time the steel blade had " turned the brandy black as ink. The steel spatula itself corroded, and when dried left a thick coating of rust, which when wiped off left a copper coat (on the spatula) almost as thick as if it had been plated with copper."

Dr. Cox warned the druggist not to sell it, and advised him not to pay for it. The New York man sued the druggist for his pay. At the trial, Dr. Cox analyzed the stuff, in the presence of the court and jury.

In one cask he found "sulphuric acid, nitric acid, nitric ether, prussic acid, Guiana pepper, an abundance of fusil oil. I pronounced it base, common whiskey. Not one drop of wine."

In the other cask he found "the same adulterations as the first, but in greater abundance, with the addition of catechu. This is most villanous."

The jury decided that the liquor was worthless, and the New York man left town without his pay. They should have decided the liquor to be criminally counterfeit, and should have sent the maker and seller of it to the penitentiary.

The druggist and other good judges had tasted out of both of these casks of brandy, and so complete was the deception that they all pronounced it a very superior article.

Taste and smell are incomplete tests. It wants a first-class chemist in every county, in all the States, with a full supply of instruments and chemicals. Let the chemists spot the base and infamous counterfeits. And let the sheriff spot the still more base and infamous counterfeiters.

You send your sons to college, and they study chemistry. Now, why don't you use their knowledge? If a lower grade of third-rate chemists mix liquors and sell receipts, why not employ first-rate chemists to expose them? Let honest, scientific chemistry expose these dishonest and sham mixtures. Why not?

But the liquor men of Cincinnati brought their influence to bear upon the next legislature of the State, so as to suppress Dr. Cox's official report.

Perhaps they will suppress this report of mine, and perhaps not. I rather think not! If it took ten thousand dollars in the legislature of Ohio, to suppress and smother down Dr. Cox's report, how much will it take to suppress and smother down these Lectures of mine?

They are going to be printed in a book, in a few days, and sold to the people, and a million of dollars will not stop them.

I shall receive nearly two hundred dollars for writing them; and it has taken about two years of labor, while I have boarded and found myself, and paid for my own paper.

Two or three years ago, a liquor house in this city offered me two hundred dollars a month, and all expenses paid, to travel on the railroads of the north-west, and sell liquors for them. I believed, and still believe, their liquors to be made chiefly of strychnine, stramonium, opium, and water, which ought to be a criminal fraud upon their customers. Of course I refused to touch them.

What! sell base, adulterated, counterfeited liquors, that I would not dare to drink myself, — made out of the organic vegetable alkalies and other poisons, — sell these to my fellow-men, for a salary of two thousand four hundred dollars a year? Not yet, not yet!

But you perhaps think these statements concerning the adulterations of liquors are not backed up with sufficient proof.

Well, I have already quoted from Dr. George B. Wood, of the Dispensatory, from the great London chemist, Frederick Accum, from the eminent educator and scholar, Eliphalet Nott, to the careful Ohio chemist, Dr. Cox, and others, and have referred you, generally, to the standard works on chemistry and medicine. But I have oceans more. I have in my possession, at this present hour, a library of some thirty or forty books and pamphlets, all of which pile evidence upon evidence tending to show the truth of all these statements. These books belong to James Black, of Lancaster, Pennsylvania, who has been buying them up, one at a time, for years.

Most of them are collections of receipts for making all kinds of liquors, and have been prepared by third-rate chemists, and experienced distillers, rectifiers, brewers, dealers, and retailers, and sold, on the sly, for enormous prices.

One of them is a book of over two hundred pages and bears the following title:

"A Treatise on the Manufacture, Imitation, Adulteration, and Reduction, of Foreign Wines, Brandies, Gins, Rums, etc., and all kinds of Domestic Liquors, based upon the French System; by a Practical Chemist and Experienced Liquor Dealer. Price ten dollars. Published for the author, in Philadelphia, 1860." This book is all it pretends to be, and bears the marks, all through it, of more than usual intelligence; and the adulterations explained in it are rather of a better grade than ordinary. This book tells you how to make one hundred and sixty-five different kinds of brandies, wines, ciders, bitters, and cordials out of common corn whiskey and cheap drugs. A whiskey man on Randolph Street, who has heard of the book, and knows that I have it, wants to give me a hundred dollars for it. He does not know where to buy another copy. Neither do I.

Another one of the books is entitled, "The Manufacture of Liquors, Wines, and Cordials, without the Aid of Distillation. Prepared and arranged expressly for the Trade." This book contains about one hundred and thirty-five receipts. Chapter VI. of this book shows how to take common raw whiskey, and make it into "brandy, peach brandy, gin, rum, cherry bounce, and all kinds of liquors, at twelve cents a gallon."

Another one is entitled, "The Brewer's and Licensed Victualler's Guide," and is similar to the two just named.

Another is entitled "Fermented Liquors," and was published in 1858.

Another is entitled "The Liquor Dealer's Guide. By a Practical Liquor Manufacturer." It was published in 1858.

Still another one is entitled "The Wine Merchant's Companion;" still another,

"The Complete Practical Distiller;" and still another, "Every Man his own Butler." These, and a number more, make up a a pretty fair liquor library.

But the meanest, vilest, and lowest of all these receipts for adulterating are not printed at all. Their base and cowardly authors have not dared to print them. These are only written on paper, hidden away, and kept securely locked. These cost money. They are studied, by candle-light, down in dingy cellars. In these you will find a depth of depravity, villany, and a heartless brutality that almost curdles one's blood. On reading these, the face of a patriot flushes and pales; and the heart of an honest man becomes posed and appalled. Are we all human? Or have some of us become demons? God forgive the wickedness of the wicked!

Thomas McMullen is the author of a book

entitled "Hand Book of Wines," which is now a text-book among the better class of grape-growers, who make smaller quantities of wine, chiefly for their own use. On page 172, he says that one wine-shipper, in a single year, shipped from Cette and Marseilles to the United States more than eighty thousand bottles of Champagne wine, "not the product of grapes, but wholly fabricated." The same author, at page 323, describes a "grape wine, that is made out of black sugar, water, and the leaves of the akaja-tree to make it intoxicating." And again he describes "English brandy that is made out of spirits distilled from corn, reduced, rectified, flavored, and otherwise drugged." And he says that "Swedish brandy is made of corn whiskey and the black ant."

Rev. Eliphalet Nott, in his Lecture No. 6, says, "I had a friend who had himself been a wine-dealer. Having read the startling statements made public, in relation to the brewing of wines, and the adulteration of liquors generally, I inquired of that friend as to the verity of these statements. His reply was, 'God forgive what has passed in my own cellar! but the statements are true, true, I assure you.'"

Now let us quote a few lines from the great English chemist, A. Normandy. This able gentleman, in the year 1850, published a book of six hundred and forty pages, entitled "The Commercial Hand-Book of Chemical Analysis." From page 95, I read these words: "Brandy, gin, rum, whiskey, etc., are alcoholic liquors, obtained from the distillation of certain fermented substances. Pure brandy is obtained from the distillation of wine, and has a pungent, agreeable taste, but barely recognizable, however, in the mixtures of alcohol and water, colored with burnt sugar, flavored with pepper, cayenne, or other acrid substances, to make believe a strength of alcohol, the proportion of which is attenuated to the least possible amount."

So that the fact that the vast majority of liquors are not what they pretend to be, but are only base imitations, is well attested. The testimony of reliable authors is almost unanimous, and cannot be disproved. The liquor men will not dare to let their slops be analyzed by competent men. It would ruin the sale of all the stock they have on hand. How can you stop the iniquitous business?

The only possible chance to detect and stop these shameful adulterations and more shameful impostors who mix them, that I can see, is to put them on the same basis with other varieties of fraud. If a man sells you a counterfeit bill for good money, what has he done? He has obtained money from you under false pretences, and by deception, — that is all. If one man forges the name of another to a note and sells it, he simply obtains money by false pretences and deception, — that is all. Now if a man sells you a liquor that is not what he pretends it is, he defrauds you out of your money, by false pretences and deception, just the same as the others; worse than the others, because he has given you, in exchange, an article that is an absolute injury to you; more so than the real liquor.

Suppose your milk-peddlers were to supply the market with milk, from cows that were trembling, falling, and dying with the terrible milk sickness that prevails in a few districts; and suppose that some of your innocent children, eating the milk, were to be poisoned to death; what would you do? You would instantly appoint first-class chemists to analyze all the milk in the market, and keep on analyzing from day to day. And, when you found a man who knowingly sold such milk, you would punish him severely. What if your butcher were to sell you beef that had died with the murrain or the rinderpest, or sell you pork that had died with the trichina or hydrophobia? Or still worse, should mix in foreign poisons, to make the meat weigh more? What would you do? You would analyze the meat and punish the wilful offender. So that, even if you believe alcoholic liquors to be as necessary as milk or meat, you should require them to be whatever they pretend to be. Afraid are you? Cowardly? Afraid to demand your rights in a land where the voice of the people rules? I guess not.

Meats, vegetables, fruits, and water are known to us all, and we can judge for ourselves; but if a man offers to sell any other kind of food or drinks, make him label the box, barrel, or bottle with the name of the contents, what ingredients compose it, and in what proportion. Analyze the contents, and if it is not what it pretends to be, — if it is a deliberate fraud, confiscate the adulterated stuff, and punish the manufacturer.

A paper currency is bad enough, but a counterfeit imitation of a worthless, irredeemable shin-plaster is worse.

But perhaps the best plan is to abolish the whole business. This course of lectures proves alcoholic liquors to be entirely worthless, and a source of great calamities and evils, and to tolerate such base imitations and poisonous mixtures of the same is a disgrace to the intelligence of this age, and a scandal to a free and moral people.

Remember, citizens, that you are free as the mountain winds, and that one wave of your mighty hand can accomplish whatever your affections desire, your intellect directs and your conscience approves. Let the principles of liberty, justice, and right remain forever, solid as the everlasting rocks, and eternal as the sea.

www.ingramcontent.com/pod-product-compliance
Lightning Source LLC
Chambersburg PA
CBHW051247300426
44114CB00011B/923